ALEXI KAYE CAMPBELL

Alexi Kaye Campbell's plays include *The Pride* (Royal Court, London, 2008; Lucille Lortel Theatre, New York, 2010; Crucible Theatre, Sheffield, 2011; Trafalgar Studios, 2013); *Apologia* (Bush Theatre, London, 2009; Trafalgar Studios, 2017); *The Faith Machine* (Royal Court, London, 2011); *Bracken Moor* (Shared Experience at the Tricycle Theatre, London, 2013) and *Sunset at the Villa Thalia* (National Theatre, London, 2016).

The Pride received the Critics' Circle Award for Most Promising Playwright and the John Whiting Award for Best New Play. The production was also awarded the Laurence Olivier Award for Outstanding Achievement in an Affiliate Theatre.

Alexi's work for film includes *Woman in Gold* (BBC Films and Origin Pictures, 2015).

Other Titles in this Series

Alexi Kaye Campbell

APOLOGIA

NICK HERN BOOKS
London
www.nickhernbooks.co.uk

A Nick Hern Book

Apologia first published in Great Britain as a paperback original in 2009
by Nick Hern Books Limited, The Glasshouse, 49a Goldhawk Road, London
W12 8QP

This revised edition published 2017

Apologia copyright © 2009, 2017 Alexi Kaye Campbell

Alexi Kaye Campbell has asserted his right to be identified as the author of this
work

Cover design by SWD

Designed and typeset by Nick Hern Books, London
Printed in the UK by Mimeo Ltd, Huntingdon, Cambridgeshire PE29 6XX

A CIP catalogue record for this book is available from the British Library

ISBN   978 1 84842 693 1

Apologia was first performed at the Bush Theatre, London, on 17 June 2009, with the following cast:

PETER	Tom Beard
KRISTIN	Paolo Dionisotti
TRUDI	Sarah Goldberg
SIMON	John Light
CLAIRE	Nina Sosanya
HUGH	Philip Voss
Director	Josie Rourke
Designer	Peter McKintosh
Lighting Designer	Hartley T A Kemp
Sound Designer	Emma Laxton

This revised version of *Apologia* was produced by Howard Panter for Trafalgar Entertainment Group, DB Productions and Dodger Theatrical, and first performed at the Trafalgar Studios, London, on 29 July 2017, with the following cast:

KRISTIN	Stockard Channing
CLAIRE	Freema Agyeman
HUGH	Desmond Barrit
TRUDI	Laura Carmichael
PETER/SIMON	Joseph Millson
Director	Jamie Lloyd
Set Designer	Soutra Gilmour
Lighting Designer	Jon Clark
Sound Designer	Ringham Bros
Associate Director	Rupert Hands

A Note on the 2017 Edition

There are two versions of *Apologia*.

When I first wrote the play, Kristin was English.

After the first production, the part started to attract the attention of a few North American actors – and we were able to cast the brilliant Stockard Channing in the 2017 London revival.

Kristin is a big and demanding role, and I knew that it would be unnecessarily challenging for an actor to play her in anything but her own native accent. I decided to then rewrite her as a woman from the States who had moved over to Europe when she was young, and made a personal and political choice to remain here.

At first I was nervous that this change would upset the play, especially the conflict between Kristin and Trudi. But when I first heard the American version read I thought that it worked equally well, but in a different way. Instead of two women separated by the differences of their national and cultural backgrounds it became the story of a woman whose past tracked her down. Trudi becomes a part of America that Kristin has been running away from but that eventually catches up with her.

This edition of the play therefore is the one with an American Kristin. Both versions of the play remain available in print.

Alexi Kaye Campbell
July 2017

For Dominic

8

Characters

KRISTIN MILLER, *American, in her sixties*

PETER, *her son, forty-ish*
TRUDI, *his American fiancée, in her late twenties/early thirties*

SIMON, *her other son, in his late thirties*
CLAIRE, *his girlfriend, in her thirties*

HUGH, *an old friend of hers, in his sixties or early seventies*

PETER *and* SIMON *may be played by the same actor.*

The play takes place entirely in the kitchen of Kristin's cottage somewhere in the English countryside, in the present.

This text went to press before the end of rehearsals and so may differ slightly from the play as performed.

ACT ONE

Scene One

The kitchen of KRISTIN's *cottage. Impressive, chaotic, eclectic – like its owner. Full of interesting and beautiful objects. The space is dominated by a large dining table.*

KRISTIN *is standing on one side of the room,* PETER *and* TRUDI *are on the other side, by the door. They have just arrived. They have two bags with them – an overnight travel bag and a large plastic one.*

PETER. Mother.

KRISTIN. Sweetheart.

PETER. We're early.

KRISTIN. You are.

PETER. No traffic.

KRISTIN. It's fine.

PETER. And Trudi wanted to see it before the sun went down.

KRISTIN. Did she?

TRUDI. The drive from London is so beautiful.

KRISTIN. As long as you don't mind me in my dressing gown.

   Pause. PETER *and* TRUDI *put the bags down.*

PETER. Mum, this is Trudi.

KRISTIN. Hello, Trudi, you're American.

TRUDI. I'm from Minnesota.

KRISTIN. I don't think Peter mentioned that.

PETER. Does it matter?

KRISTIN. Not in the least.

TRUDI. I've heard so much about you. And I've read your work.

KRISTIN. It's just a little ironic, that's all.

PETER. How is it ironic?

KRISTIN. I'm an American too, Trudi.

TRUDI. I know that.

KRISTIN. By birth, not choice. I left the US when I was twenty-two and have made my life in Europe. But America always has a way of tracking me down.

TRUDI. I'm not a drone missile, Mrs Miller.

KRISTIN. Of course you're not, you look far too sweet. Call me Kristin.

Slight pause.

We have a bit of a crisis on our hands.

PETER. What kind of crisis?

KRISTIN. I need you to look at the oven, sweetheart.

PETER. The oven?

KRISTIN. It just doesn't feel to me like it's getting hot enough.

PETER. Have you got something in there now?

KRISTIN. Chicken.

TRUDI. Okay.

PETER. I thought I told you Trudi was a vegetarian.

KRISTIN. There's potatoes. And vegetables, of course.

TRUDI. I love potatoes.

KRISTIN. But I can't remember you telling me she was a vegetarian, or an American.

TRUDI. Really, Kristin, it's fine.

PETER *opens the oven.*

PETER. It's not that hot.

KRISTIN. And I've put it on full.

PETER. What time is it?

TRUDI. Just turned six.

KRISTIN. I mean we won't be eating for at least another hour so maybe –

PETER. It doesn't feel that hot in there.

KRISTIN. Can you look at it?

PETER. Look at it?

KRISTIN. I mean check the electrics, that kind of thing. It might be a switch.

PETER. It's not a switch and no, I can't look at it. I mean I wouldn't know where to start. You need an electrician.

KRISTIN. Tonight of all nights. I wanted everything to be –

PETER. What's your contingency plan?

KRISTIN. Contingency plan?

PETER. I mean if it doesn't get any hotter. Pasta, or something?

KRISTIN. The hobs seem to have gone as well. I tried them earlier. I was thinking I could poach it or something. As a last resort. Cut it up and fry it.

PETER. Fry the chicken?

KRISTIN. But the hobs seem to have gone as well. The whole damn thing.

PETER. So what do we do?

KRISTIN. I could drive it over to Phil and Lou's. Borrow their oven.

PETER. That's twenty miles away.

KRISTIN. I know that.

PETER. You can't be driving up and down the motorway with a chicken in the back seat.

KRISTIN. Or we could just have a cold meal. I'm sure I could be inventive. Forage for food in the cupboards, you know. Look for things.

PETER. Look for things?

KRISTIN (*looking in the cupboard*). There's anchovies, nuts.

PETER. Nuts?

KRISTIN. I have a cos lettuce in the fridge.

PETER. We're not bloody squirrels.

KRISTIN. Make a salad, you know.

PETER. Anchovy nut salad?

KRISTIN. Be inventive is what I mean.

TRUDI. I love salads.

KRISTIN. It's still early. It'll probably warm up.

PETER. Unlikely.

KRISTIN. We won't be eating for another hour.

PETER. It's broken.

KRISTIN. So in the meantime let's just try and be positive, shall we?

PETER. We'll try.

KRISTIN. And I'm sure you didn't tell me Trudi was a vegetarian.

PETER. My version of events against yours.

A slightly awkward pause.

KRISTIN. I was just about to make some coffee.

PETER. Okay.

KRISTIN. But I think under the circumstances a glass of wine would be more appropriate.

TRUDI. That would be lovely.

KRISTIN. Good.

PETER. I'll do it.

PETER *gets three glasses out of a cupboard and a bottle of wine out of the fridge. It is already uncorked – maybe* KRISTIN *has had a glass before they arrived.*

TRUDI (*remembering*). Oh, happy birthday.

PETER. Of course.

KRISTIN. Thank you.

TRUDI. Shall we...?

PETER. What?

TRUDI. You know...

PETER. Oh.

TRUDI. Should we...?

PETER. Oh that.

TRUDI. We've brought you something.

PETER. Maybe we should wait.

TRUDI. Or you could open it now.

She opens the plastic bag she's brought with her and takes out quite a large, strangely shaped object, which is wrapped in paper.

KRISTIN. Oh my God, what is that?

TRUDI. Happy birthday.

KRISTIN. It's big.

TRUDI. It's from somewhere far away.

KRISTIN. How exciting.

TRUDI. I hope you like it.

KRISTIN. Shall I open it now?

PETER. Go on then.

KRISTIN. Okay, if you insist.

She starts to unwrap it. PETER *has poured the three glasses of wine.*

TRUDI. We kind of chose it together.

PETER. Trudi chose it.

TRUDI. I thought it was very, very beautiful.

PETER. She sort of fell in love with it.

TRUDI. And I said to Peter, maybe your mother will love it too. I knew it was kind of risky but –

PETER. But we took the chance.

TRUDI. And we really hope you like it.

KRISTIN *has taken the paper off and the object is revealed – an African tribal mask. It is beautiful and disturbing the way these masks can often be – it has an exaggerated long face and a very broad forehead.* PETER *has handed* TRUDI *her glass of wine but holds on to* KRISTIN's *because she is holding the mask.*

KRISTIN. A mask.

TRUDI. Yes.

KRISTIN. An African mask.

PETER. It's from Liberia.

TRUDI. When Peter was there and I went with him. He was working all day and I was stuck in the hotel watching CNN.

KRISTIN. A tribal mask.

TRUDI. I was kind of nervous of going out on my own.

KRISTIN. It's extraordinary.

TRUDI. We were in Monrovia.

PETER. The capital.

TRUDI. But there's only so much TV you can watch. So Peter was out all day with the people from the bank meeting with all these guys from the government. And I got bored. So I ventured out.

PETER. Not on your own.

TRUDI. With this guy from my hotel who was like my bodyguard or something. Peter arranged it. It was crazy.

KRISTIN. You needed a bodyguard?

TRUDI. And we just walked around this marketplace and then this woman suddenly came up to me. She was very, very

beautiful and quite young but when she opened her mouth I
noticed she had no teeth. I mean not a single tooth. It was kind
of freaky. Anyway, she grabbed me by the arm and asked me
to stay there and she ran into her house and then came out with
this mask and said that she would sell it to me. And I kind of
fell in love with it.

PETER. And the next day she took me over and showed it to me
and persuaded me to buy it.

TRUDI. For you. Because I knew you liked beautiful objects of
art. And of course it's the real thing, what I mean is it's not like
the ones they sell at the airport. It's the real thing.

A pause as KRISTIN *takes in the mask.*

I really hope you like it.

KRISTIN *continues to examine it.*

KRISTIN. It's a tribal mask.

TRUDI. Yes.

KRISTIN. It's definitely impressive.

TRUDI. Oh, I'm so glad you like it.

KRISTIN. But what's its significance?

TRUDI. Its...?

KRISTIN. Its significance, history, function, its life.

TRUDI. How do you mean?

KRISTIN. Which tribe does it belong to? Was it made to conjure
rain out of the sky or to bring punishment to those who had
transgressed?

TRUDI. I don't –

KRISTIN. Did the person who wore it dance a dance of delirium
so as to be taken over by the spirit of an ancestor or to pray for
the crops?

TRUDI. I don't know –

KRISTIN. Or perhaps to bring famine and death to his enemies?

TRUDI. I really don't know. She didn't say.

KRISTIN. I suppose what I'm saying is that these objects – these strange, mysterious objects – are steeped in their own histories and we know very little of them so to expatriate them in exchange for a few hundred dollars seems a little –

PETER. Mother.

KRISTIN. It's not that I'm superstitious because I'm not. I just suppose I wish I knew something of the context in which it was created. Because its main purpose was definitely not decorative. So for it to be here, in this house, as a decorative object seems to be... how can I put this... disrespectful, I suppose. Both of it and of the artist who created it.

PETER *gives her a look.*

But thank you. It's very kind.

TRUDI. I just thought it was beautiful.

KRISTIN. It is. It is. It is.

TRUDI. And I thought that –

KRISTIN. Somewhere in my study I have a book on African tribal art. We'll have a look later. See if there's any point of reference. Not my area of expertise I'm afraid. So we'll have a look at the book.

TRUDI. That would be good.

KRISTIN. But thank you.

TRUDI. Happy birthday.

Pause. KRISTIN *places the mask down on one of the kitchen counters somewhat awkwardly as if she is uncomfortable with it. It stares out at them for the rest of the evening.* PETER *hands her the glass of wine.*

I was wondering...

KRISTIN. Yes?

TRUDI. I need to powder my nose.

KRISTIN. Of course you do. Through the door on your right.

TRUDI. Thank you.

> TRUDI *leaves the room. A short pause.* KRISTIN *takes some napkins out of a drawer and starts to fold them.*

KRISTIN. She's pretty. Why didn't you tell me she was from the States?

PETER. Be nice to her.

KRISTIN. It doesn't bother me, it's just weird, that's all. All those nice English girls and you show up with an American. It's a little Oedipal, sweetheart.

PETER. Jesus Christ.

KRISTIN. Not that she's like me in any way.

PETER. Couldn't be more different.

KRISTIN. Anyway, at least she's the right age.

PETER. What do you mean?

KRISTIN. You know. Children.

PETER. For fuck's sake.

KRISTIN. Well you have to think about these things. If you want a family, honey.

PETER. We're in love.

KRISTIN. She looks fertile.

PETER. I want you to be nice to her.

KRISTIN. Like a Minnesotan peach tree.

PETER. I don't believe this.

KRISTIN. And she's got that look.

PETER. What look?

KRISTIN. Like she's going to be a good mother.

PETER. How d'you mean?

KRISTIN. Some women just have it. It's in the eyes.

PETER. The eyes?

KRISTIN. The eyes that say I'm going to be a good mother.

Pause.

I've missed you.

PETER. Yes.

KRISTIN. It's been –

PETER. I've been busy.

KRISTIN. How's that awful bank you work for?

PETER. The bank is fine.

KRISTIN. Still raping the Third World?

PETER. Brutally.

KRISTIN. I was thinking that in the present climate your job would have lost some of its allure. I keep hoping you're going to pack it all in and grow your own vegetables. Teach maths to kids. Anything. You've always looked awkward in a suit. Then I can be proud to call you my son again.

PETER. Please don't moralise. You know nothing about what I do.

KRISTIN. I know you're with the takers and not the givers.

PETER. Enough.

Pause.

How's Simon? Is he coming?

KRISTIN. Claire said she'd pick him up after filming. But you don't really know these days, do you?

PETER. Know what?

KRISTIN. She said he disappeared for three days last week. She called the police.

PETER. Fuck.

KRISTIN. I think she was implying he'd been living rough.

PETER. Living rough?

KRISTIN. On the streets, under the bridges, God knows.

PETER. Jesus.

KRISTIN. The point is, Peter, your brother is having a complete mental breakdown and the sooner we start recognising it for what it is the better it is for all of us.

PETER. I suppose.

KRISTIN. He's left his job.

PETER. When did that happen?

KRISTIN. On Thursday.

PETER. The café?

KRISTIN. Three jobs in as many months.

PETER. Shit.

KRISTIN. He said he needs the time to work on his novel.

PETER. Okay.

KRISTIN. He's been working on his novel for seven years.

Pause.

PETER. And Claire?

KRISTIN. What about her?

PETER. What's she doing about it?

KRISTIN. Nothing.

PETER. Nothing?

KRISTIN. She's a soap actress, Peter.

PETER. What's that got to do with it?

KRISTIN. I'm convinced she's driven him to it in the first place. There's something *missing* in her.

PETER. Missing?

KRISTIN. You try living with a big gaping hole in close proximity. Must be unnerving I would imagine.

PETER. Claire's not the problem.

KRISTIN. Isn't she?

PETER. No.

KRISTIN. I just want him to be happy.

Pause.

PETER. I read your book.

KRISTIN. Oh?

PETER. It made me...

KRISTIN. What? It made you what?

TRUDI *comes back.*

PETER. Hey.

TRUDI. I love your bathroom. All those books. And that beautiful picture of the old man over the toilet.

KRISTIN. That's Karl Marx.

TRUDI *picks up her glass of wine.*

TRUDI. You have such a wonderful house, Kristin. It's so artistic.

KRISTIN. Thank you.

TRUDI. Peter had said you had great taste.

KRISTIN. Is that what he said?

TRUDI. And of course I knew you were a famous art historian.

KRISTIN. I wouldn't go that far.

TRUDI. Well your books are on sale in all the major bookstores.

KRISTIN. Oh well, in that case.

TRUDI. When Peter and I were in New York there was like one of those island things in Barnes and Noble on Fifth Avenue dedicated to the memoir. And they had like a big picture of you mounted on cardboard.

KRISTIN. How impressive.

TRUDI. I have been quite nervous about meeting you. But you're a lot nicer in real life. Nicer than your cardboard version.

KRISTIN. A little more animated I hope.

TRUDI. Definitely.

Pause.

KRISTIN. I need to turn the hot water on. I wasn't expecting you till at least seven.

PETER. You said.

KRISTIN. And I want you to change that bulb for me. The one I mentioned on the phone.

PETER. I'll do it now.

KRISTIN. I don't like standing on that stool. My balance –

PETER. I said I'll do it.

KRISTIN. Back in a second.

KRISTIN *leaves the room.* PETER *walks over to* TRUDI *and puts his arms around her.*

PETER. What do you think?

TRUDI. She's amazing.

PETER. And?

TRUDI. She hates the mask.

PETER. No.

TRUDI. I thought she'd like it.

PETER. I don't think she hates it.

TRUDI. I really thought she'd like it.

PETER. Maybe she just needs time.

TRUDI. Time?

PETER. You know, to get used to it. It's that kind of thing, isn't it?

TRUDI. What kind of thing?

PETER. Kind of thing you need time for it to grow on you. She'll end up loving it. You'll see.

Pause.

TRUDI. Why does she have a picture of Marx in the bathroom?

PETER. She's an old Commie. Having said that, poor old Karl used to hang over the stairs but was recently demoted to the downstairs loo.

TRUDI. I've never met a Communist before. Especially an American one. I thought they were all dead.

PETER. Well, she's not really... I mean, it was more of a phase, and a lot of it was done for show.

TRUDI. She doesn't strike me as the kind of person who'd pretend to be something she wasn't.

PETER. She's a bloody nightmare.

TRUDI. Don't say that, she's your mother.

PETER. Opinionated, didactic, dictatorial.

TRUDI. I don't see that.

PETER. Okay.

He kisses her.

My brother's coming, hopefully.

TRUDI. I can't wait to meet him.

PETER. He's been having a rough time.

TRUDI. You said.

PETER. As usual.

TRUDI. How do you mean?

PETER. Things just never seem to stick.

TRUDI. Stick?

PETER. They never have.

TRUDI. Poor Simon.

PETER. He's been trying to write.

TRUDI. It must be difficult.

PETER. It is.

TRUDI. He sounds fragile.

PETER. And now...

TRUDI. What?

PETER. He feels broken I suppose.

Pause.

I love you.

TRUDI. I love you too, Petey-poo.

Pause.

Will we tell them before or after the meal?

PETER. Let's see.

TRUDI. See what?

PETER. See how it all goes.

TRUDI. I thought after would be nice. Maybe dessert. And then we'll have champagne. Her second birthday present.

PETER. Maybe.

TRUDI. Please, Petey.

PETER. Okay. We'll see.

KRISTIN *comes back, light bulb in hand.*

KRISTIN. Here it is.

PETER. I'll do it now.

KRISTIN. Thank you, darling.

PETER. And I'll put our bag in the room.

KRISTIN. You're in the yellow one. I've left towels on the bed.

PETER *takes the bulb from her, leaves the room and takes their overnight bag with him.* KRISTIN *goes to the oven, opens it.*

Do you know, it feels like it's getting ever-so-slightly warmer.

TRUDI. That's hopeful.

KRISTIN *goes and opens a cupboard and takes out some plates.*

Can I help you with anything, Kristin?

KRISTIN. I suppose you could help me set the table. We'll need to eat something whatever the outcome. The cutlery is in there.

TRUDI. Sure.

During the next few moments the two women set the table together – mats and plates with cutlery and then the glasses.

KRISTIN. So what about you, Trudi? What brought you over here?

TRUDI. Oh, I'm doing a Physiotherapist Masters Course at Brunel.

KRISTIN. And how did you meet my son? Through friends or at a party, or something?

TRUDI. Oh, no, we met at a prayer meeting.

KRISTIN *stops in her tracks; a little as if she's just been slapped in the face.*

KRISTIN. A what?

TRUDI. A prayer meeting. It was Peter's first. A mutual friend of ours brought him along. A girl called Sarah who works at the bank with him. She was at high school with me.

KRISTIN. A prayer meeting?

TRUDI. Well, that's what they call it but actually it's more of a get-together. It's really quite social. I mean there is a little prayer but mostly people talk about their lives. And have coffee and biscuits.

KRISTIN. How do you mean, a prayer meeting?

TRUDI. A Christian prayer meeting.

KRISTIN. A Christian prayer meeting?

TRUDI. Yes.

KRISTIN. So you're a Christian?

TRUDI. Most of the people who go to the Christian prayer meetings usually are.

KRISTIN. And Peter?

TRUDI. I'm sorry, I'm being facetious. But yes, Kristin, Jesus is an important part of my life.

KRISTIN. I'm thrilled for you. But what was my son doing there?

TRUDI. I just think he came to see what it was like.

KRISTIN. Okay. Wow.

TRUDI. Does that surprise you?

KRISTIN. He's just never really been in to all that.

TRUDI. In to?

KRISTIN. Please tell me he hasn't been speaking in tongues.

TRUDI. He hasn't been speaking in tongues.

KRISTIN. In to religion. That's one thing I thought I got right.

TRUDI. Have you never had faith, Kristin?

KRISTIN. Loads of it. And I believe in mystery, imagination and the power of myth and metaphor. But not in outmoded patriarchal propaganda.

TRUDI. That's interesting. Where are the glasses?

KRISTIN. That cupboard there. Just put some of the plain ones out, for water. Oh and some flutes for the champagne. You can leave those on the counter.

TRUDI *opens the cupboard and starts bringing the glasses to the table.*

I'm slightly shocked. Money's been more Peter's thing.

TRUDI. Well maybe this is a reaction against that.

KRISTIN. I don't know which is the worst of the two.

TRUDI. That makes me sad.

KRISTIN. All of a sudden the idea of him keeping the whole of sub-Saharan Africa in crippling debt doesn't seem quite as bad a proposition.

TRUDI. I don't think you mean that.

KRISTIN. Please don't tell me what I mean.

A slightly awkward pause. They continue laying the table.
TRUDI *works hard at winning her back but* KRISTIN's *mood has taken a turn.*

TRUDI. He's really been looking forward to coming. To see you, I mean.

KRISTIN. Oh?

TRUDI. He talks about you a lot.

KRISTIN. I'm surprised.

TRUDI. You've obviously played a very big part in his life.

KRISTIN. I am his mother.

TRUDI. Of course.

KRISTIN. Parents, you'll find, generally have a way of doing that. Playing a big part in your life.

TRUDI. It's true.

KRISTIN. It's less of a talent and more of a God-given right. So please forgive me if I'm not overtly enthusiastic in responding to what I assume was intended to be a compliment.

TRUDI. I didn't mean…

KRISTIN. But I'm glad to hear he talks of me. Fondly or with hatred?

TRUDI. Something's happening to Peter.

KRISTIN. Happening?

TRUDI. I have to tell you, Kristin, that ever since I've known him I feel that Peter is a man on the brink of quite important change in his life.

KRISTIN. I'm almost certain you're implying that has something to do with the grace of our Lord Jesus Christ.

TRUDI. Like he's asking all these questions he's never asked himself before. And maybe this new curiosity is just one symptom of that journey.

KRISTIN. God, I hate that word. It's so American.

TRUDI. Well, I am American. Both of us are, Kristin.

KRISTIN. That may be the case. But at least one of us is aspiring towards a vocabulary that avoids the kind of cliché found on the blurb of a self-help manual.

TRUDI. Things are changing in America, Kristin. We've just elected our first African-American president. It's exciting.

KRISTIN. That is a good thing, it's true. But let's wait and see how things turn out in the long run before we start jumping with joy.

She realises that she's gone too far.

I'm sorry, I just. I've been taken by surprise, that's all. My son, the born-again Christian.

TRUDI. He told me you were a passionate woman.

KRISTIN. Did he?

TRUDI. But I like you. I like you a lot.

KRISTIN. Lucky for you. Otherwise this evening would be most unpleasant.

TRUDI. He did warn me.

KRISTIN. Good.

Pause. They have finished laying the table. They sip their wine. KRISTIN warms a little to make up for her barbed comment.

You're pretty.

TRUDI. Thank you.

Pause.

It must have been a little scary coming here on your own when you were just twenty-two.

KRISTIN. Some of it was. But I was hungry for a challenge, Trudi. I also wanted an ocean between my mother and myself.

TRUDI. Sometimes you need to get away to discover who you really are.

KRISTIN. So I came here with a few clothes and a few books and a will to reinvent myself. I stepped out of that damn Connecticut corset she had forced me into and I danced, and smoked weed and made love to many people and went to Paris and Rome and Morocco. It was a glorious time and anything and everything felt possible, my dear.

TRUDI. That must have been so exciting.

KRISTIN. And then I met the boys' father. He was dashing, and angry and wrote dark poems and I fell in love with him.

TRUDI. I wish I'd met him. It's such a shame he died.

KRISTIN. People do.

TRUDI. Peter hasn't told me all that much about him.

KRISTIN. He loved his boys, I'll give him that. A decent father.

And the memory of him changes her mood again. She puts her glass down, stands. The moment between them is over.

He was also irascible, moody, manipulative.

TRUDI. I'm sorry.

KRISTIN. I'm trying to be objective.

TRUDI. That's funny.

KRISTIN. Emotionally stunted, mentally cruel, chauvinistic and very, very lucky.

TRUDI. Lucky?

KRISTIN. Even in death he was lucky. He had a massive stroke. It took him thirty-six seconds to die. The bastard.

TRUDI. That's quick.

KRISTIN. Much to my disappointment he escaped the joys of self-reflection on a deathbed.

TRUDI. You must be very angry with him.

KRISTIN. Oh no, I've let it go. I used to be but it was killing me.

TRUDI. Kristin. Forgiveness is such a liberating emotion.

KRISTIN. I'll bear that in mind.

Pause. TRUDI *is trying to tread carefully.*

TRUDI. Peter told me about the divorce.

KRISTIN. Did he?

TRUDI. It must have been difficult for you.

KRISTIN. What was?

TRUDI. I mean… what happened. You know.

KRISTIN. I haven't a clue what you're talking about.

TRUDI. Peter told me about…

KRISTIN. Yes?

TRUDI. Peter told me about the separation.

KRISTIN. Separation?

TRUDI. It must have been very painful losing your children. Not watching them grow up. How old were they when he took them away from you? Nine and seven?

There is a pause and TRUDI *realises that she has overstepped the mark.*

Things were so different then, weren't they?

Pause. KRISTIN *doesn't respond.* TRUDI *is working hard.*

I think we take things for granted nowadays is what I'm saying. Women, I mean.

KRISTIN. Do you?

PETER *returns.*

PETER. Done.

KRISTIN. Thank you, sweetheart.

PETER. Anything else?

KRISTIN. Not that I can think of.

Slight pause. PETER *walks over to the fridge and opens it. Pours himself another glass of wine.*

Trudi and I have been talking.

PETER. That's good.

KRISTIN. Trudi was telling me about your prayer meetings.

PETER. Oh that.

TRUDI. Your mother was a bit surprised that you came along, Peter.

PETER. She would be.

KRISTIN. Just a little surprised that you're looking for God.

PETER. Mother calls herself a humanist.

KRISTIN. The word 'prayer' on its own is bad enough. When it's a prefix to the word 'meeting' it's absolutely terrifying.

PETER. You were very much one for meetings in your youth, Mother.

KRISTIN. They were not religious. They were political.

We were not worshipping some big illusion in the sky.

PETER. Only yourselves.

KRISTIN. It was more of a case of putting your house in order because you care about it as opposed to putting it in order because that big bad landlord up above is watching your every move.

PETER. Is that what it was?

Pause.

TRUDI. I read your book, Kristin. It's wonderful.

PETER. Sweetie.

KRISTIN. I'm flattered.

TRUDI. I'd never really read your work so when Peter took me to Florence a few weeks ago I thought it was a good opportunity. It was very thrilling for me to be able to read about your life while being surrounded by the places and art that inspired you. Not only in Florence but Assisi too. It was fascinating. And your book was informative and inspiring.

KRISTIN. What a rich array of adjectives.

TRUDI. It must have been amazing spending seven years there. In Florence I mean.

KRISTIN. It had its moments.

PETER. I told her about your flat overlooking the Arno.

TRUDI. And your passion for Giotto. Of course all of that is in the book.

KRISTIN. I was working.

PETER. And hanging out with Italians.

TRUDI. And I kept asking myself, I mean when we were there, when I was looking at his work, I kept asking myself what it was about him, I mean about that particular artist, that grabbed you so. Why him and not the others. I mean I realise that he was the first one, I realise that he was the father of the Renaissance...

KRISTIN. And mother...

TRUDI. But I kept thinking why him and not the others? What it was about him in particular that moved you so?

Pause.

KRISTIN. Let's have a top-up. And then I'll have my shower. Trudi? More wine?

TRUDI. Thank you.

KRISTIN. Good.

She walks to the fridge and gets out the bottle of wine and refreshes their glasses.

Did you read the book, Trudi?

TRUDI *throws a quick, confused glance over at* PETER.

PETER. Mother.

KRISTIN. Because surely, if you read it properly, if you applied yourself, the answer to your question would be somewhat obvious.

TRUDI. I didn't mean to...

KRISTIN. Surely, if my book is half as good as you say it is, you wouldn't really need to ask that question because the answer would be self-evident.

TRUDI. Maybe I didn't quite understand all of it.

KRISTIN. Maybe.

> KRISTIN *pours wine into* TRUDI*'s glass and then into her own.*

TRUDI. It's a whole new territory for me, Kristin. Art history I mean. I've never really studied it before.

KRISTIN. He was a revolutionary. He took religious iconography and completely transformed it.

TRUDI. Okay.

KRISTIN. Let me tell you a story, Trudi, and maybe this will answer your question more effectively than three hundred and seventy-five pages seems to have done.

PETER. Not now.

KRISTIN. Imagine you are living in the early years of the fourteenth century in some small village a few miles outside Padua. You're in your early thirties but you look sixty-five because you work in some field all hours of the day and at night you have to care for a family of nine...

TRUDI. That's a big family.

KRISTIN. Including a husband who regularly and happily beats you. Four of your children have died in childbirth. Your fingers are constantly blistered and you smell of your own sweat. Despite the brutal conditions of your life however you happen to be a sensitive and inquisitive soul.

TRUDI. Okay.

KRISTIN. You are constantly reminded by the wonderful Catholic Church that just in case you ever entertained the thought of patting yourself on the back for surviving this horrible adversity, you are in fact a bad, carnal creature, intemperate and steeped in original sin. As a matter of fact you're also constantly reminded that in all likelihood you will end up in some crowded furnace being prodded by all sorts of objects including pitchforks and dog's genitalia whilst surrounded by flesh-eating goblins and assorted whores and perverts.

TRUDI. How disturbing.

KRISTIN. As a consolation, and some sort of carrot you are also offered an alternative but this alternative is strange and foreign to you. These two-dimensional, alien figures stare down at you with absurd expressions, set against a gold backdrop. They don't look remotely human. They are supposed to promise some sort of an afterlife but it all stretches your credulity because they reflect nothing familiar and gold is a colour reserved for the rich, those who have paid for a place in this hallowed heaven through patronage. That much you've sussed out. Brown is more your colour, the colour of the clumps of earth you dig out with your hands every day and the colour of your shit. Then suddenly one day this funny thing happens.

TRUDI. A funny thing?

KRISTIN. You are in a chapel and you kneel down to pray. This is an acquired habit, something you were taught to do from infancy and even though you do it with some feeling there is a question that accompanies that feeling and the question, which fills you with shame and fear is whether the receptor of your prayer, in all His might and power will be able, in all truth, to understand and commiserate with your petty needs, your small and humble pains. This thought brings you out of your meditation and your eyes drift upwards to just one part of a giant fresco that adorns the vaulted ceilings above you: an image of the Madonna cradling the body of her son in her arms. Your eyes move further up slowly, curiously, taking in the soft skin, the nape of the neck, the gentle contours of the face and then... then you actually stare at the face for the first time and a chill runs up your spine and your whole view of life changes for ever. The Madonna's expression is one of anguish and loss, her mouth tilted slightly upwards as if she is asking the same questions that you are, her left hand touching her son's neck as if trying to stroke him back to life. You realise now that this face is not only recognisable – the face is yours. *Your* weeping eyes, *your* pale cheeks, *your* mouth that slightly curls with doubt. It's a mirror. That's all. But all of a sudden your whole perspective changes and maybe things become a little more bearable. Someone else has connected with you and you discover the meaning of the word *empathy*. With that you begin to realise that you are part of a collective experience. You will perhaps continue to pray but in a completely new way. Your prayers will be directed more to something within yourself, a nascent capability. And the knowledge that you carry that within you gives you a little strength. And a little reassurance.

TRUDI. That's beautiful.

KRISTIN. That's why I love Giotto, Trudi. That's humanism emerging from the religious matrix. Evolving. He was the first who did that. The vision, the power and the responsibility of the artist. The rest is superstition.

Pause.

TRUDI. Thank you for welcoming me to your home. You're an interesting and extraordinary woman.

KRISTIN. This hyperbole has to stop.

Pause.

TRUDI. And the book's title.

KRISTIN. The title?

TRUDI. *Apologia.*

KRISTIN. What about it?

TRUDI. It's one of those words. Like you think you know what it means but then maybe you don't. Or at least what you think it means is not exact. Not precise. *Apologia.*

KRISTIN. It means a formal, written defence of one's opinions or conduct.

TRUDI. Okay.

KRISTIN. Not to be confused with an apology.

Pause.

I'm off to have my shower.

PETER. Okay.

KRISTIN. Why don't you take Trudi to the bottom of the garden. Show her the magnolia tree and the view over the hills. It's the right hour of the day for it.

TRUDI. That sounds wonderful.

KRISTIN. And then I suppose we'll have to solve the problem of what exactly it is we're going to eat tonight in the unfortunate event of that fucking oven not getting its act together.

She puts her wine glass down on one of the counters and makes a move towards the door. But just as she gets to it she turns around. She looks at PETER.

Your face has changed.

PETER. My face?

KRISTIN. I was looking at you just now when the sun caught it.

PETER. How has my face changed?

KRISTIN. And I thought he's not a boy any more.

PETER. Congratulations for noticing. Not for about twenty-five years now.

KRISTIN. He's not a boy.

A pause and for a minute she's lost in thought. And then she brings herself back.

Welcome.

She leaves the room.

Blackout.

Scene Two

An hour later. PETER *and* TRUDI *are standing in the kitchen with glasses of wine in hand. They have been joined by* CLAIRE *and* HUGH, *who are also drinking.* CLAIRE *is wearing an expensive-looking, light-coloured dress.*

TRUDI. It really is so wonderful to meet you, Claire. I've heard so many things about you.

CLAIRE. You have?

HUGH. Your reputation precedes you, my dear.

TRUDI. About your career I mean. Your acting.

CLAIRE. Oh that.

TRUDI. It sounds so exciting.

CLAIRE. It has its moments.

TRUDI. Peter was saying you're quite famous.

CLAIRE. Comes with the territory I'm afraid.

TRUDI. That's fun.

CLAIRE. I'm a very private person so I don't enjoy all that. I miss my anonymity.

HUGH. You do?

CLAIRE. Of course I like being appreciated for my work.

TRUDI. Everybody does.

CLAIRE. But fame was never my objective.

HUGH. Of course not.

Slight pause.

TRUDI. So what's the soap opera about? Where's it set?

CLAIRE. Sorry?

TRUDI. Peter mentioned in the car that you were in a soap opera and I'm just wondering what it's about.

CLAIRE. Oh.

TRUDI. I mean the kind of world it takes place in.

CLAIRE. Well, it's not really a soap opera.

HUGH. Isn't it?

CLAIRE. Not really. Not technically.

PETER. Oh, I'm sorry.

CLAIRE. It's more of a serialised drama that happens to follow the trajectories of various people's lives.

HUGH. A *what*?

CLAIRE. It's just a different genre is what I'm saying.

HUGH. A different genre?

CLAIRE. But it's about the lives of these people who work in an advertising agency.

HUGH. How thrilling.

CLAIRE. Their relationships, their works, their dilemmas.

They're seriously good scripts.

TRUDI. I'm sure.

CLAIRE. Subtle and ambitious.

TRUDI. What a great job.

CLAIRE. They have depth.

Pause.

As a matter of fact, I had some good news yesterday.

TRUDI. You did?

CLAIRE. They've just renewed my contract for another year.

TRUDI. That's great.

PETER. Well done.

CLAIRE. Thanks, Peter.

HUGH. Who's a clever girl.

CLAIRE. I did have a moment. Do I really want to do this for the rest of my life, I asked myself.

HUGH. And then you thought, 'Why ever not?'

CLAIRE. I've had to turn down quite a bit of theatre work.

HUGH. Have you?

CLAIRE. But I weighed everything up and decided that it's the right thing to do.

TRUDI. Congratulations.

CLAIRE. Because it really is quite classy.

Pause. Suddenly HUGH *spots the African mask.*

HUGH. Oh, my God what is that thing?

PETER. It's a mask –

TRUDI. That Peter and I bought Kristin –

HUGH. It's hideous.

TRUDI. As a gift.

HUGH. And beautiful at the same time. You know how some things have that ability to be hideous and beautiful at the same time? It's fascinating.

CLAIRE. Did you get it at that shop behind the British Museum?

TRUDI. No, it's the real thing.

CLAIRE. Taboo or something. Just off Russell Square.

PETER. It's from Africa.

TRUDI. Liberia. We bought it in Liberia.

CLAIRE. Coz it looks very much like the ones that they sell at that shop.

TRUDI. It's the real thing.

HUGH. Extraordinary.

Pause.

So how's our boy?

CLAIRE. Not good.

PETER. I heard.

TRUDI. Poor Simon.

CLAIRE (*slightly monitoring the volume of her voice*). Your mother's book.

PETER. What about it?

HUGH. The memoir?

CLAIRE. I think that's what she calls it.

TRUDI. She writes so beautifully.

CLAIRE. He finished it this morning.

PETER. Oh?

CLAIRE. He said the strangest thing after he'd read it.

PETER. He did?

CLAIRE. 'Why did she have children?' That's all he said.

HUGH. That is strange.

CLAIRE. He just threw it across the room and said, 'Why the fuck did she have children?'

KRISTIN enters the room. She is showered and dressed.

KRISTIN. Why did who have children?

HUGH (*thinking on his feet*). Anna Karenina.

KRISTIN. Anna Karenina?

CLAIRE. We were talking about books.

HUGH. Nineteenth-century Russian literature.

KRISTIN. I see.

CLAIRE. And I was just asking why Anna Karenina had bothered having children –

HUGH. If all she wanted was to shag Vronsky.

CLAIRE. That's all.

KRISTIN. That's an interesting reading of it.

She kisses HUGH *on the cheek.*

I've made a bed for you. In case you want to have a few drinks and stay the night. You and Simon are in the green room, Claire.

HUGH. Thank you, darling. And by the way we've ordered the Chinese.

KRISTIN. I'm so embarrassed.

HUGH. Don't be. We're all rather relieved at having avoided death by poultry.

KRISTIN. It's not my fault that damn thing broke down.

A pause as she realises SIMON *isn't there.*

Where's Simon?

CLAIRE. He might be joining us later.

KRISTIN. What do you mean, he might be joining us later?

CLAIRE. I came straight from the studio –

KRISTIN. I thought the whole point was that you were going to pick him up and bring him here.

CLAIRE. I was. But then we spoke on the phone and –

KRISTIN. And what did he say?

CLAIRE. He said he couldn't make his mind up.

KRISTIN. Couldn't make his mind up about what?

CLAIRE. He was being monosyllabic.

KRISTIN. He's depressed.

CLAIRE. I know. I live with him, Kristin.

KRISTIN. So he's not coming?

CLAIRE. He said he might drive over later.

KRISTIN. Maybe we should try calling him.

CLAIRE. I just did. He didn't answer.

KRISTIN. As long as he's not drinking.

CLAIRE. I'm his girlfriend, Kristin.

KRISTIN. I just thought that you were going to bring him here safely.

CLAIRE. Not his babysitter.

CLAIRE *takes a gift-wrapped box out of her bag and hands it to* KRISTIN.

But happy birthday anyway.

KRISTIN. This is for me?

CLAIRE. It's just a little something. Oh, and I've brought a cake. Mango meringue. It's in the fridge.

HUGH. Mango meringue?

KRISTIN. I wasn't expecting anything.

HUGH. How delicious.

CLAIRE. Open it.

KRISTIN starts to unwrap the present.

TRUDI. I love watching people opening presents.

HUGH. I know what you mean. Especially that priceless moment when they have to conceal their disappointment behind an inane grin.

KRISTIN has unwrapped the gift – a jar of cosmetic cream – and an expression very similar to the one just described by HUGH is etched on her face as she reads the writing on the box.

KRISTIN. 'TRANSFORMATIVE REJUVENATION'.

HUGH. Just in the nick of time.

CLAIRE. It really is a miracle-worker. They only sell it at Selfridges. There's a waiting list. My mother swears by it.

KRISTIN. How kind.

CLAIRE. I was torn between that and the new Virginia Woolf biography. But I read a stinking review in the *Observer* so I got you the face cream instead.

KRISTIN. Much more useful, I'm sure.

CLAIRE. Enjoy. And keep it in the fridge.

KRISTIN. You really shouldn't have.

HUGH has gone to the fridge and he pops open a bottle of champagne.

TRUDI. That's my favourite sound in the world.

HUGH. Good girl.

TRUDI. I always associate it with celebration. And I love celebrations!

She goes over to where HUGH *is standing and helps him with the champagne – holding up the glasses one by one for him to pour it into and then handing them out to everyone. As she does this,* HUGH *is holding up his glass in a toast. He camps it up.*

HUGH. And this evening we are celebrating the birthday of the legend that is Kristin Miller. Pioneer of Arts and Letters, Champion of the Voiceless and Redemptive Saviour of the Western World.

TRUDI. That's funny.

HUGH. Over the years we have watched you evolve from feisty American nymph to placard-wielding activist, from alarmingly coiffed Courtauld post-graduate to even more alarmingly coiffed hippy bride. In your pursuit of the common good you have offered yourself to as many causes as I've had social diseases. From the back streets of Palestine to the the Parisian barricades you have made your presence felt most emphatically –

PETER. In some quarters.

HUGH. And most importantly, with your passionate, often lambasted contribution to the traditionally male-dominated bastion of art history you have always done things – and this is where I get serious and maybe even a little teary-eyed – with a whole load of *heart*. Tonight, Kristin Miller, we salute you.

CLAIRE. We salute you.

They all raise their glasses, though PETER *is a little unenthusiastic.*

TRUDI. Happy birthday.

KRISTIN. Thank you, thank you, thank you. Very heartfelt if a little over-the-top, darling.

HUGH *is suddenly holding a small wrapped gift which he presents to her.*

HUGH. And here is a little something to go with my well-rehearsed eulogy. Not quite as essential as Transformational Regeneration –

CLAIRE. Transformative Rejuvenation.

HUGH. But a gift nonetheless of rare and priceless significance. At least to me.

He hands over the gift and she begins to unwrap it.

I was clearing out some old shoeboxes in my study the other day. Found it in there in amongst a heap of CND pamphlets and a whole lot of yellowed news clippings. It made me laugh.

She has unwrapped it and the object has revealed itself. It is a beautifully framed photograph. KRISTIN *lets out a shriek of recognition and excitement when she sees it.*

KRISTIN. I love it!

HUGH. Isn't it extremely fabulous?

TRUDI. What is it?

KRISTIN. We look so young.

HUGH. We *were* young. And fucking gorgeous.

KRISTIN. And high on everything under the sun!

CLAIRE. Can I see?

They all start to crowd around KRISTIN *to look over her shoulder at the photograph.*

HUGH. With our lives stretched in front of us like scrolls waiting to be written upon in indelible ink.

TRUDI. That's so poetic.

HUGH. And our eyes glittering with the possibilities of all our tomorrows.

PETER. Jesus.

CLAIRE (*looking at the photograph*). That is hilarious.

HUGH. And our hearts thumping in anticipation of forthcoming sexual encounters.

TRUDI. You look so beautiful.

HUGH. Thank you, Trudi. She's not bad either, is she?

KRISTIN stretches out her hand, grabs HUGH by his.

KRISTIN. Thank you for this, I'll treasure it.

Pause.

TRUDI. Where was it taken?

HUGH. Appropriately enough at a demonstration.

KRISTIN. *The* demonstration, against the Vietnam War. We marched to the US Embassy.

HUGH. In Grosvenor Square. Threw some eggs at the embassy gates and then ate the rest back at mine with an awful bottle of plonk.

PETER. What fun.

KRISTIN. It was. Oh my God, look, just behind you, it's Gustavo, the Chilean guy, I loved him. And there's Melissa... what was her name?

HUGH. Melissa Jones. A feminist poet with a gift for subtlety. Her first anthology I believe was entitled *Devil Penis*.

KRISTIN. I remember that floral shirt. People whistled at you in the street.

HUGH. I was provocative in my youth. Madam was halfway through her masters degree. She was a clever thing with a shocking amount of self-confidence.

PETER. Of course.

KRISTIN. We stayed up all night and then went down to the coast in the morning and swam in that freezing sea. Gustavo sang all those Chilean songs on the beach, remember?

HUGH. The two of you made quite a pair.

KRISTIN. And then I dragged him off to some other protest.

HUGH. I suppose we just wanted to change the world. At least your mother did. She stood somewhere between reactive anger and the new hedonism like a beacon.

KRISTIN. I also happened to be having a hell of a lot of fun, remember.

PETER. I'm sure.

HUGH. But you really did want to transform the world in a more permanent way, so don't pretend you didn't. Political to her core and fuelled with anger. And I kind of tagged along for the ride. I was a follower, like a fucking disciple. The woman was persuasive.

PETER. She always is.

CLAIRE. That's hilarious.

KRISTIN puts the framed photograph down somewhere in the room and it joins the tribal mask in staring out at them for the rest of the evening.

TRUDI. Photographs are such beautiful things. I mean I know that sounds obvious but all I mean is maybe it's one of the many things we take for granted. To hold the past in your hand like that, just like you were, Kristin, to hold the past in your hand and look at it and remember what it was like to be young – the clothes, the friends, the many dreams you had. To hold the past in your hand as if it were a ball or a little mirror or something, to hold it as if...

She suddenly realises she's getting a little carried away and loses her confidence.

To hold the past in your hand.

HUGH. I really rather like you, you know.

TRUDI. Thank you.

Pause.

KRISTIN. So what was it exactly that you found hilarious, Claire?

CLAIRE. Sorry?

KRISTIN. Twice you used the word hilarious. Once when you saw the photograph and then a second time a minute ago when Hugh said something kind about what drove me. And I'm just wondering what exactly it was that you thought was hilarious. Why the use of that specific word.

CLAIRE. Oh, you know, the sixties, the early seventies. Everything about it. The clothes, the hair, the raging idealism. It's sweet.

KRISTIN. Sweet?

CLAIRE. The thought of you all marching in your sandals. The bandanas, the CND logos, 'make love not war', the braided flowers, the whole damn thing. *The answer my friends is blowing in the wind.* I love it.

HUGH. It was rather wonderful.

CLAIRE. I just have this image of you all sprawled out in Hyde Park with daisies in your hair, planning ways to overthrow the government.

PETER. Or smoking Gauloises on the Left Bank as you dipped your toes in the ocean of student revolt.

KRISTIN. Dipped our toes?

CLAIRE. Until you could afford a Bang and Olufsen stereo system and a house in the suburbs.

Pause.

That was a joke.

PETER. I know what you mean though.

CLAIRE. But at least you're the real thing, Kristin. I mean you've given *everything* you have and don't think we haven't noticed.

PETER. Everything.

CLAIRE. Because you have all these other people, these sixty-eighters or whatever you want to call them who go around as if they'd personally fought on the side of the Viet Cong or single-handedly brought civil rights to America and then you find out that what they really mean is that they used to shop at Biba.

Pause. HUGH grabs the bottle of champagne and starts to top up the glasses.

HUGH. Who's for more bubbly?

CLAIRE. Thanks, Hugh.

TRUDI. Lovely, thank you.

PETER. Thanks.

He empties the bottle and rests it on the counter.

KRISTIN. I really am worried about Simon you know.

CLAIRE. We all are, Kristin.

KRISTIN. No, but I mean tonight. I'm especially worried about him tonight. Knowing that he's quite happy to have a few drinks and jump behind the wheel of his car –

CLAIRE. He'll be fine.

KRISTIN. Knowing that, I'm really quite surprised that you didn't make sure he got here safely –

CLAIRE. I keep thinking he's like one of those buildings.

KRISTIN. Buildings?

CLAIRE. In Iran, God knows, Turkey.

KRISTIN. How is he like a building in Turkey?

CLAIRE. When there's an earthquake. And of course it's the earthquake that does it – I mean that's what does the damage, that's the thing that brings the building down, that kills the people inside.

HUGH. What *are* you talking about?

CLAIRE. But then they find out corners were cut. In the construction of it. Shoddy work, that kind of thing. The edifice was weak.

PETER. The foundations.

KRISTIN. I'm not quite following this analogy.

CLAIRE. I think all I'm saying is that I'm worried too, Kristin.

PETER. Of course you are.

CLAIRE. But enough said.

The doorbell rings.

TRUDI. Maybe that's him.

HUGH. That'll be the chop suey.

PETER. That's quick.

KRISTIN *takes her purse out of her bag and starts to make her way out of the room.*

HUGH. Don't even think of paying, it's on me.

KRISTIN. Don't be ridiculous, you can't afford it.

HUGH. For fuck's sake, woman, it's your birthday.

KRISTIN. You're very, very poor.

HUGH. I've asked you not to bring that up in public.

KRISTIN. Anyway, you're a guest.

HUGH. I'll bloody fight you for it.

He follows her out of the room.

TRUDI. They're very lovely.

PETER. That's one way of putting it.

CLAIRE. Such a double act.

PETER. Symbiotic.

Pause. They know KRISTIN *and* HUGH *are in the next room so the next few lines are spoken quietly.*

CLAIRE. It's weird timing, I'll give her that.

PETER. Timing?

CLAIRE. The book, I mean.

PETER. Oh.

CLAIRE. I just hope it's not the straw that breaks the camel's back.

PETER. I'm livid.

CLAIRE. I mean it says it on the back, doesn't it? It actually says something like 'the life and times of'.

PETER. That's what it says.

CLAIRE. So to call it that and then not even mention you. To not even mention that she ever had children.

PETER. It's weird.

CLAIRE. As if you didn't exist. It's a little spooky.

PETER. Stalinist more like.

CLAIRE. I couldn't quite get my head round it. I mean what was she thinking?

PETER. Fuck knows.

CLAIRE. I mean it's hurtful.

TRUDI. Maybe she was –

CLAIRE. It's just a very strange choice. And I can understand you both feeling very...

PETER. What?

CLAIRE. Wounded, I suppose. Betrayed.

PETER. I need to talk to her.

TRUDI. But not tonight please, Petey.

Pause.

I'm sure there's an explanation. I'm sure she didn't mean to upset you. Sometimes people behave in the strangest ways and there's usually a reason.

PETER. Maybe.

KRISTIN *and* HUGH *return with a bag of Chinese food.*

HUGH. The witch wrestled me to the ground.

KRISTIN. You didn't give me a choice.

HUGH. With her nasty protruding claws.

TRUDI. That smells delicious.

KRISTIN. We should just shove it in the oven and wait till Simon gets here.

PETER. The oven's kaput, remember.

KRISTIN. I don't want us to start without him.

PETER. Which is why we're not eating your chicken in the first place.

HUGH. Thank heaven for small mercies.

PETER. And if we wait the food will just get cold.

KRISTIN. I just think we should wait.

PETER. And we don't want to eat cold Chinese.

HUGH. We don't.

PETER. So we don't really have a choice.

CLAIRE. I'll just make sure we put some food aside for him, Kristin.

PETER. I think we should eat.

HUGH. I'm famished.

TRUDI. Me too.

KRISTIN. Help yourselves.

KRISTIN *starts taking the cartons out of the bag, opening them and placing them on mats in the middle of the table. There is a general commotion for the next few minutes as they all hover round the table in preparation to sit down. They are all talking at the same time, almost overlapping.*

TRUDI. Can I do anything to help?

KRISTIN. You could just get some serving spoons out of that drawer.

TRUDI. Sure.

TRUDI *opens the drawer and gets serving spoons out, which she then brings to the table and places by the cartons of food.*

KRISTIN. Peter, there's red over there if anyone wants any.

HUGH. White is good.

CLAIRE. I think I'll have red.

PETER. Honey?

TRUDI. Can I have red, sweetie?

PETER. Sure.

PETER *gets a bottle of white wine from the fridge and a red one from the cupboard, which he uncorks. They all start taking their seats around the table. There is much movement and again, the conversation almost overlaps. Once they sit,*

KRISTIN *ends up at the end of the table, with an empty seat opposite her which is for* SIMON.

TRUDI. That is such a beautiful dress, Claire.

CLAIRE. Thank you. I splashed out on it.

TRUDI. It's beautiful.

KRISTIN. You splash out on yourself a lot, don't you.

CLAIRE. It's true, I confess.

TRUDI. I'm sure you deserve it.

PETER. Where shall we all sit?

KRISTIN. Anywhere you like.

TRUDI. Is it from a designer store?

HUGH. You sit at the end, birthday girl, like the queen that you are.

CLAIRE. It's Tomako Mihara.

TRUDI. Tomako who?

HUGH. Imperatrix Kristina.

PETER. Sweetie, why don't you sit opposite me?

TRUDI. Okay, honey.

HUGH. Regina Terribilis, reigning over her dominions.

CLAIRE. Tomako Mihara, she's a new Japanese designer.

TRUDI. I've never heard of her.

HUGH. Overseeing the lands of her subjects with a steely eye of disapproval and despair.

TRUDI. I'm not really familiar with designers. I don't really read *Vogue* or anything.

CLAIRE. No?

HUGH. And wondering where it all went horribly wrong.

TRUDI. I mean I've heard of Gucci and stuff.

PETER. Are we using these spoons to serve with?

KRISTIN. We are.

TRUDI. But I don't generally know a lot about fashion.

PETER. That's one of the things I love about you.

TRUDI. Though I do know a beautiful dress when I see one.

CLAIRE. That's very kind, thank you, Trudi.

They are all serving themselves the food.

TRUDI. This smells so delicious.

PETER. These are veggie, sweetie.

TRUDI. Thanks, honey.

CLAIRE. This really is a treat.

HUGH. What's that one?

CLAIRE. Beef in oyster sauce or something.

HUGH. Something weird is floating in it.

CLAIRE. I can't see anything.

HUGH. Like a fingernail or something.

TRUDI. A fingernail?

HUGH. Or maybe I'm just imagining things.

CLAIRE. Oh no, I see it, I see it too.

PETER. This one doesn't have meat in it either.

TRUDI. Thanks, sweetie.

PETER. Sure, honey.

CLAIRE. I think I'll give that one a miss.

Pause.

KRISTIN. So how much does a dress like the one you're wearing
now set you back then, Claire?

CLAIRE. I never divulge my secrets.

KRISTIN. Two hundred pounds? Three hundred?

TRUDI. That's a lot of money.

PETER. Why do you want to know how much her dress costs?

CLAIRE. I had an especially bad week at work so I decided to spoil myself.

KRISTIN. Good for you.

CLAIRE. It was just very stressful.

HUGH. Down the mines.

CLAIRE. And I said to myself, 'You know what, Claire? You deserve this.'

TRUDI. I'm sure your work can be quite gruelling.

KRISTIN. All those lines to remember.

CLAIRE. So I splashed out.

TRUDI. Sometimes it's good to do that.

KRISTIN. How much?

CLAIRE. Two thousand.

TRUDI. Pounds?

HUGH. Fuck me sideways with a bargepole.

KRISTIN. Trudi's looking rather pale.

TRUDI. No, I'm not I –

HUGH. That's like the GDP of Angola.

KRISTIN. Maybe she's re-evaluating whether you deserve it or not.

CLAIRE. And you know what, I don't feel guilty.

KRISTIN. Obviously not.

CLAIRE. I just think to myself, 'I've worked hard for this, I've paid my dues, I survived drama school, I've had my time out of work and if I want to spend two thousand pounds on a Tomako Mihara dress –

TRUDI. It really is very beautiful.

CLAIRE. – then I will. I fucking will.'

KRISTIN. Congratulations.

CLAIRE. Cheers.

The beeping of a mobile-phone text message. PETER *starts to check his pockets.*

PETER. Was that me?

TRUDI. It didn't sound like yours, honey. It was more birdy.

CLAIRE. I think that was mine. Excuse me.

She stands up and starts looking for her handbag.

HUGH. This is delicious.

KRISTIN. It sounded like mine.

TRUDI. Aren't you going to have some rice, sweetie?

KRISTIN. Two thousand pounds for a piece of clothing.

PETER. I'm okay, sweetie.

CLAIRE *sees a phone on the kitchen counter and picks it up.*

CLAIRE. Whose is this?

KRISTIN. I think that one's mine.

HUGH. God knows why you have one. You don't even know how to fucking use it.

CLAIRE. That's weird. It's just like mine.

KRISTIN. Peter chose it for me.

CLAIRE *is rummaging through her handbag looking for her phone.*

CLAIRE. I'm sure it was mine. I just want to check in case it's Simon.

TRUDI. Hugh, can you pass me that one there please?

HUGH. The one with the fingernail in it?

TRUDI. No, the one next to it. The pak choi.

He hands it over to her. CLAIRE *has found her phone and reads the text.*

CLAIRE. It is from Simon.

KRISTIN. Is he on his way?

CLAIRE. That's weird.

PETER. What does it say?

CLAIRE. 'Coming over. Need to talk to her.'

KRISTIN. Talk to who?

CLAIRE. That's all it says.

KRISTIN. I expect he means me.

HUGH. That sounds ominous.

> CLAIRE *puts the phone down on the counter, right next to*
> KRISTIN*'s, and then sits down at the table again.*

TRUDI. Oh you know what, we should have another toast.

PETER. What for, sweetie?

TRUDI. For Claire. For the renewal of her contract.

KRISTIN. What contract?

CLAIRE. Never mind.

TRUDI. Claire has been asked to do another year of the serialised
drama she's in.

CLAIRE. It's really not very –

KRISTIN. The what?

TRUDI. And she's just accepted so I think it's fitting that we raise
our glasses to her and congratulate her.

KRISTIN. The soap?

TRUDI. Well, Claire was saying that it's not really a soap.

KRISTIN. It isn't?

TRUDI. That it's more of a –

CLAIRE. It's fine, Trudi, really it's fine. But thank you.

PETER. Yes, congratulations.

CLAIRE. Thank you, Peter.

TRUDI. So I thought we should have a little toast.

They all raise their glasses.

HUGH. Cheers. May you continue to grace our television screens with your compelling trajectories.

KRISTIN. What trajectories?

PETER. Cheers, Claire.

CLAIRE. Thank you, Peter.

HUGH. Now if you'll excuse me I'm going to fish out the offending fingernail.

He picks up the carton of food and peers into it with his fork poised.

TRUDI. Have you ever watched it, Kristin?

KRISTIN. The soap?

HUGH (*still looking for the fingernail*). It's disappeared.

TRUDI. Well, yes.

CLAIRE. Simon made her once. Strapped her to the chair kind of thing.

HUGH. It seems to have submerged itself into the oyster sauce.

CLAIRE. Not really your thing, was it, Kristin?

KRISTIN. The camera loves your face.

CLAIRE. Thank you.

KRISTIN. But I remember finding it misanthropic.

TRUDI. Misanthropic?

CLAIRE. Told you.

HUGH (*serving himself from the carton*). Fingernail or not, I'm going to be brave and eat some.

KRISTIN. It was a little vacuous. I kept asking myself, 'Why do people watch this? And why do they make it?'

PETER. Maybe because it's entertaining.

KRISTIN. I suppose it's a question of making money. It's about product.

CLAIRE. Here goes.

KRISTIN. Aspirational, isn't that the word? Everybody wears wonderful clothes in it. The women especially are so beautiful. Criminally superficial and always ready to hop into bed with the boss but definitely beautiful.

HUGH. Sounds a corker.

CLAIRE. At least not everybody agrees with her. It's won awards and the ratings have gone through the ceiling.

TRUDI. How exciting to be a part of that.

CLAIRE. It is.

KRISTIN. I'm not surprised. It's definitely alluring in a way. Accessible and hypnotic.

CLAIRE. And I think the writer is a real genius. He's kind of glamorising the whole world but subverting it at the same time.

KRISTIN. I must have missed that.

CLAIRE. It's full of irony.

PETER. It sounds great, Claire.

CLAIRE. But it's never obvious.

KRISTIN. No.

PETER. We'll look out for it next week.

Pause.

HUGH. I'd avoid this one if I were you. It tastes a little funny.

PETER. Sweetie, can you pass me the chicken?

TRUDI. Sure, honey.

She passes him the chicken dish.

CLAIRE. I wonder what Simon wants to talk to you about.

KRISTIN. I'm sure we'll find out.

A slight pause as they all eat.

TRUDI. And do you ever act in the theatre?

CLAIRE. I have acted on stage, yes.

PETER. We came to see you in *A Doll's House* once, didn't we?

CLAIRE. That's right.

KRISTIN. In Camden. Over that pub.

CLAIRE. You were very supportive.

HUGH. Over a pub?

CLAIRE. It was Off-West End. A fringe venue. But one of the ones with a really good reputation.

TRUDI. I'm sure.

KRISTIN. There was an overwhelming smell of deep-fried scampi.

CLAIRE. I played Nora.

TRUDI. I don't really know the play.

KRISTIN. But you were very good in it, I remember.

CLAIRE. Thank you, Kristin.

KRISTIN. The direction was a little funny. The concept. It was set in a meat factory or something.

PETER. The actors were throwing food at each other.

HUGH. Good God.

PETER. And everyone was wearing leather aprons.

HUGH. How exciting.

KRISTIN. But whatever the production is like just to hear that play is enough.

TRUDI. I really wish I'd seen it.

KRISTIN. Groundbreaking.

HUGH. Isn't it though?

PETER. You were very good in it.

CLAIRE. Thank you, Peter.

Pause.

TRUDI. Claire, can I ask you a question?

CLAIRE. Of course.

TRUDI. I mean it's probably the most stupid, unoriginal question you've ever been asked along with 'how do you learn your lines?' but I really want to know the answer so I'm not just asking in a flippant way or to pass the time.

CLAIRE. Go ahead.

TRUDI. But why did you become an actress? I mean what was it that made you choose that particular path in life?

CLAIRE. Okay.

HUGH. She likes the frocks.

KRISTIN. That's not a stupid question, Trudi. It's the most important question anyone can ever ask her.

TRUDI. What was it that made you say to yourself one day, 'This is what I want to do for the rest of my life'?

KRISTIN. And I want to hear the answer too. Because what motivates people fascinates me.

Pause. All eyes on CLAIRE.

CLAIRE. I suppose it's coz I always enjoyed telling stories.

TRUDI. Stories?

CLAIRE. When I was a little girl I used to enjoy dressing up –

HUGH. Told you.

CLAIRE. And telling stories. And I suppose I enjoyed it so much that I decided to do it for the rest of my life.

KRISTIN. But I think what Trudi's really asking you is what makes you want to tell stories in the first place.

TRUDI. Well, I wasn't really –

KRISTIN. Is it because you are trying to communicate something which will in some direct or indirect way improve the world in which you live, point it towards a better understanding of itself –

CLAIRE. Well, I suppose –

KRISTIN. Or is it simply that you enjoy the sensation of having all eyes on you a great deal of the time?

CLAIRE. It's a combination of both, Kristin.

TRUDI. That makes sense.

CLAIRE. I feel ever so slightly that I'm being interrogated.

PETER. You are.

KRISTIN. But which is your raison d'être. Your existential propeller if you like. Is it the will to live in service of some larger whole –

HUGH. I'm assuming that 'whole' with a 'W' before the 'H'.

KRISTIN. Or is it an exercise in narcissism?

HUGH. Though living in service of a hole without a 'W' before the 'H' also sounds like a rather attractive proposition.

KRISTIN. Because it really is an interesting question.

Pause.

CLAIRE. It's the first. I'm an artist.

KRISTIN. And I remember that night, that even if the production misfired in certain ways, there was something about sitting in that room watching you compete with the sounds of thumping bass drum and the smell of cheap food –

TRUDI. That must have been really challenging.

KRISTIN. Speaking words that had been written a hundred years before which questioned everything about the established order of the day, everything of what it meant to be a woman at that particular point in time, that there was something beautiful about it and strangely moving.

HUGH. But why were they throwing food at each other?

KRISTIN. Which brings us back to the subject of your current work. The soap.

CLAIRE. Here we go.

KRISTIN. And I have to now repeat, within the context of this particular conversation, that it is the biggest pile of putrid shite I have ever seen in my life.

HUGH. Don't hold back, darling.

CLAIRE. We know how you feel about it, Kristin, and I'm sorry that it's not your thing but I think as I explained earlier I don't happen to agree with you. I think it's a clever and profound piece of television.

KRISTIN. Surely you can't mean that.

PETER. Why can't she?

KRISTIN. Because that's an even more frightening thought than you doing it just for the money.

HUGH. Do you know, I'm feeling ever so slightly queasy.

CLAIRE. You really are unbelievable.

KRISTIN. That would be understandable, doing it for the money.

PETER. Why can't you just respect the fact that people don't always see things the way you do?

HUGH. I think it was the beef thing.

PETER. Why can't you just respect that?

HUGH. I think I may have swallowed that fucking fingernail.

CLAIRE. I just don't think you get it. Maybe it's a generational thing.

KRISTIN. *That* I could understand.

CLAIRE. I mean it is aimed at younger people and maybe there's something about it –

KRISTIN. Most people have been whores at some point in their life.

CLAIRE. That you simply don't get.

HUGH. I really do feel rather sick.

Pause.

CLAIRE. I'm sorry, did you just call me a whore?

Pause.

HUGH. And ever so slightly dizzy too.

TRUDI. Maybe you're just allergic to Chinese food.

HUGH. Or Chinese fingernails.

TRUDI. The monosodium glutamate.

Pause.

CLAIRE. And yes, of course I need the money as well, Kristin. I need to make a living. To survive.

KRISTIN. And drive a Porsche.

CLAIRE. But that doesn't negate the fact that I think it's a good piece of work.

KRISTIN. Our capacity for self-delusion is phenomenal, Claire.

PETER. That's rich.

CLAIRE. And I'm fucking proud of it if you really want to know.

KRISTIN. I'm sorry but it's something I feel quite passionate about.

HUGH. Obviously.

KRISTIN. The misappropriation of words.

PETER. What misappropriation of words?

KRISTIN. It's just that she said she was an artist.

CLAIRE. That's right, I am an artist.

KRISTIN. And I just don't know what that means any more. To be an artist.

CLAIRE. Don't you?

KRISTIN. I mean you may laugh at this, you may find it sweet and hilarious but an artist was someone whose voice could be the instigator of social change. And that it's that voice that we hang on to in some way to save us from the rampant stupidity of religion on the one hand and vacuous consumerism on the other.

HUGH. I really think I'm going to be sick.

KRISTIN. So to waste that or to sell it to the highest bidder really seems to me like the worst possible betrayal.

TRUDI. I'll get you a glass of water, Hugh.

TRUDI stands, but as she does she knocks over the bottle of red wine which spills all over the place but mostly onto CLAIRE's dress.

Oh my God. Oh my God. I am so sorry... I am so –

CLAIRE *is in shock.*

HUGH. Sweet Jesus. That's an expensive accident.

TRUDI. I am so sorry, Claire, I am so terribly sorry –

CLAIRE. It's fine, really it's fine.

PETER. It was an accident, sweetie.

TRUDI. I am so terribly, terribly sorry.

CLAIRE. I said it's fine.

TRUDI. Here let me...

She picks up a bottle of water, pours some onto a napkin and starts dabbing the dress with it.

Maybe if we soak it.

CLAIRE. I don't think that's doing any good.

HUGH. Try salt.

CLAIRE. I really don't think that's doing any good.

HUGH. You need to put some salt on it.

TRUDI (*who keeps dabbing her with water*). I'm so sorry, I'm so sorry, I'm so sorry.

CLAIRE. Trudi, please.

PETER. Sweetie, leave it.

HUGH. Why don't you put some fucking salt on it.

PETER. I don't think salt will do any good, Hugh, it needs to go to the dry cleaner's.

TRUDI. Maybe Hugh's right.

TRUDI grabs the salt dispenser which stands in the middle of the table and starts to sprinkle it very liberally and rather hysterically onto CLAIRE's *dress.*

Maybe this will do it.

CLAIRE. I really don't think –

TRUDI. I just stood up too quickly –

PETER. It was an accident –

TRUDI. And the bottle was right next to the edge –

CLAIRE. I really don't think you covering me in salt is going to make that much of a difference –

TRUDI. And it all just happened so quickly –

CLAIRE. The point is the dress is fucked.

TRUDI. But I'm so terribly sorry.

CLAIRE *(forcefully)*. So please stop doing that. Stop covering me in salt.

TRUDI. I feel really awful.

CLAIRE. BECAUSE I'M NOT A FUCKING PIECE OF MEAT.

Pause. TRUDI *is slightly taken aback, as is everybody else.*

PETER. It was an accident.

CLAIRE. I'm sorry. I didn't mean –

TRUDI. No, I'm sorry.

PETER. She's just trying to help.

CLAIRE. I didn't mean to snap at you, I'm sorry.

TRUDI. No, I'm sorry.

CLAIRE. It really isn't your fault.

KRISTIN. I bet you now wish you'd invested that two thousand pounds in a slightly wiser way.

Pause. CLAIRE *takes a deep breath and turns to face* KRISTIN.

CLAIRE. How dare you criticise my choices? How dare you sit there in judgement on me?

KRISTIN. I only do it because I expect more from you.

HUGH. That's slappable, darling.

KRISTIN. Because you are my son's partner and I like to trust his judgement.

CLAIRE. You're a fucking dinosaur, Kristin.

KRISTIN. However challenging that may be.

CLAIRE. I'll tell you something though. When you do eventually talk to Simon, or rather when he talks to you, tells you what it is, why it is, what the fuck it is that has driven him to this strange, dark place he now finds himself in –

KRISTIN. It's some of the choices you've made that I have problems with –

CLAIRE. If you choose to listen for once in your life, I mean really listen –

KRISTIN. Not the person you are.

CLAIRE. Well, maybe then you'll be in for a surprise. An unpleasant surprise or two.

KRISTIN. I'm simply saying that as an artist and as a partner you are taking the route of least inconvenience to yourself but the route of most peril to others.

CLAIRE. You are fucking unbelievable.

KRISTIN. The one thing one could say in your favour is that at least you're consistent in your lack of commitment to the things which are the most imperative.

PETER. I think you're barking up the wrong tree.

KRISTEN. Concepts, stories, human beings – *my son*.

PETER. I said I think you're barking up the wrong fucking tree.

KRISTIN. Consistent in your profound inability to give a fuck about anyone other than yourself.

PETER. I said YOU'RE BARKING UP THE WRONG FUCKING TREE.

TRUDI. Sweetie, please.

There is a pause as they're all taken aback by this sudden explosion.

KRISTIN. Why am I barking up the wrong tree, darling?

PETER. Let's talk about your book, Kristin.

KRISTIN. It always makes me nervous when you start calling me Kristin.

PETER. Let's talk about your fucking book.

TRUDI. Sweetie.

CLAIRE. Your *memoir*.

A pause. KRISTIN *stands up and starts to clear up the plates.*

KRISTIN. I'll start clearing these up and then maybe we can have some of that cake you brought, Claire.

HUGH. I can't say I'm in the mood for mango meringue.

PETER. The way you write about art is thrilling.

TRUDI. It really is a wonderful book, Kristin.

PETER. The supporting characters however seem a little sketchy.

KRISTIN. The supporting characters?

PETER. I myself happen to be a little more thick-skinned shall we say but if I were Simon – if I were my brother Simon whose skin perhaps has never been quite as thick as mine – whose *soul* has never been quite as resilient –

CLAIRE. It hasn't.

PETER. I might ask myself how in a book that calls itself a memoir, that purports to be your fucking life story, I don't get a single fucking mention.

CLAIRE. Not one.

PETER. I am your son, I would say to myself, I would have liked to have played a slightly more pivotal part in what I'm sure it describes on the back flap as 'the life and times of'. Would that be churlish of me?

CLAIRE. He was devastated.

KRISTIN. It's a work memoir. I wasn't interested in airing my dirty laundry.

PETER. Fuck me, now she's calling us dirty laundry.

TRUDI. I don't think that's what she means, honey.

PETER. That awful Italian you shacked up with for a couple of years got a whole fucking chapter.

KRISTIN. Only because he was the foremost Renaissance-painting restorer of his generation. But I'm sorry if you felt the book *neglected* you in some way.

PETER. And I have to now ask you the question I have been leading up to, the question I have been secretly asking myself for many, many years, the question that has been gnawing in my fucking chest since I was a small boy, the same question I've just been informed your other son is also keen to hear the answer to.

TRUDI. Sweetie, please.

KRISTIN. Go on then.

PETER. And the question is why did this woman have children if she wasn't prepared to do the job properly?

Pause.

And I honestly don't think that Claire being in a soap opera is the problem here.

TRUDI. It's not a soap opera, sweetie.

Another pause and KRISTIN *quietly tops up her glass with wine.*

KRISTIN. Have you finished?

HUGH. Hopefully.

PETER *doesn't answer.*

KRISTIN. You know nothing.

PETER. Tell me then.

KRISTIN. Not now. Not like this. Not like a witch-hunt.

She continues to put things away, clearing up, piling plates up on the counter. Nobody speaks and the others remain seated.

I'm going to bed. If Simon does show up, tell him I'll see him in the morning.

Nobody speaks. She moves towards the door, then stops and turns to look at PETER *and* CLAIRE. *She directs her words to both of them.*

You know nothing about what it means to live for something slightly larger than yourselves so anything I say in my defence will sound like a foreign language to you. I don't know how, I don't know *why* this happened but somewhere along the line earning money – for the most part at the cost of other people's suffering – seems to have become your only objective. And I honestly think, Peter, that this new religious path you've decided to follow is just a way of assuaging what can only be a troubled conscience. Of course taking responsibility for your actions would release just as many endorphins as swaying in the pews does. The only difference is that they'd be a slightly better class of endorphins. You'd have earned them.

PETER. What the fuck has that to do with anything?

KRISTIN. I could sit here for twenty-four hours and try and describe to you what it means to be *political*, what it means to fight for something other than your own material and domestic wellbeing and you wouldn't understand. We could debate on what defines a good parent through the night and still we wouldn't agree. But yes, I'm sure that in *your* version of what constitutes a good mother you are right that I have failed you in every possible way.

PETER. You have.

KRISTIN. But more than anything what appalls and depresses me is that you have never once asked yourself – not really, not *honestly*, Peter – what it might have been like for me. Then, I mean. In Florence. When he took you away from me. In that way, you have persistently shown a quite catastrophic failure of imagination. Your father would be proud of you.

Suddenly, CLAIRE's mobile rings.

That'll be Simon.

Thinking it's her phone, KRISTIN answers it.

Hello?

CLAIRE. I think that's my phone, Kristin.

There is a pause as KRISTIN listens to someone on the phone.

I said I think it's mine.

KRISTIN (*on the mobile*). I believe it's Claire you want to talk to.

CLAIRE. Who is it?

KRISTIN (*still on the mobile*). Please don't apologise, it's been informative and entertaining.

CLAIRE. Can I have my phone please?

KRISTIN. Well, it isn't Simon.

She walks towards CLAIRE, mobile in hand.

But whoever it is said he's booked the room for Thursday night and he can't wait to fuck you up the arse.

She hands the mobile to CLAIRE.

Goodnight, everyone.

She leaves the room. CLAIRE is left holding the mobile.

CLAIRE. It isn't... it's a friend... it's not... it really isn't what it... the thing is...

Pause as she realises she's losing a battle.

Fucking bitch.

She storms out of the room, mobile in hand.

HUGH. Lucky girl.

TRUDI. I wish I'd never asked her why she wanted to be an actress.

PETER. It's not that, sweetie.

Pause.

HUGH. What did she mean when she called her a dinosaur?

Pause.

Excuse me, but I think I'm going to be sick.

HUGH *rushes out of the room as if he is about to be sick.*

PETER *and* TRUDI *are left alone. There is a pause and then* TRUDI *starts to quietly cry.*

PETER. Trudi?

TRUDI. I'm sorry I –

PETER. Sweetie?

TRUDI. I'm sorry. I'm just a little emotional that's all. It's just that –

PETER. Of course you are –

TRUDI. It's just that I wasn't expecting this.

PETER. Neither was I.

TRUDI (*through her tears*). And everything you said made me so sad, so very, very sad and I started thinking about poor Simon and then earlier when your mother was talking to me about Giotto, about what he did as an artist, I mean about how he changed the world, how he *transformed* the way we looked at each other and that made me quite emotional too, I don't know why but it did, it kind of all made sense and then I started thinking, later, when she was talking about art and about everything like that, and what she just said now about responsibility, I started thinking about Jesus about what it is about him that I love so much, about why it is I'm a Christian and I had a terrible thought that what if the only reason I like

Jesus, I love Jesus is just because... because... is just because...

PETER. Because what?

TRUDI. Is just because he makes life simpler.

PETER. Oh, sweetie.

TRUDI. And I ruined her Japanese dress.

PETER. Honey.

TRUDI *runs out of the room in tears.*

Jesus.

He runs after her.

The room is empty. Then SIMON *enters. He is wearing his coat and looking slightly dishevelled. His right hand is bleeding and he has wrapped a handkerchief around it. He looks around the room as if wondering where everyone has disappeared to. He sits at the table.*

Blackout.

End of Act One.

ACT TWO

Scene One

The middle of the night, a few hours later. The food has all been cleared away. SIMON is sitting at the table with KRISTIN. SIMON is fully dressed but KRISTIN is in her dressing gown. He has taken the handkerchief off his hand and KRISTIN is inspecting his palm.

KRISTIN. There's definitely some in there.

SIMON. Okay.

KRISTIN. Little pieces of glass. Tiny splinters.

Pause.

We'll have to get them out.

SIMON. Fine.

KRISTIN. How did you do it?

SIMON. I got off the train. I was walking down the road looking for a cab. It was raining.

KRISTIN. Claire should have brought you here.

SIMON. I was trying to do up my shoelaces. There was broken glass in the undergrowth by the road. I lost my balance and fell on it.

KRISTIN. There's definitely some in there.

SIMON. It could have been worse.

KRISTIN. So let's get it out.

She stands and walks over to a cupboard. She opens it and takes out a first-aid kit.

I've been looking forward to the day this thing would come in handy.

She brings it over to where he's sitting. She sits down and opens it. She starts to take out all the contents of the box, laying them out carefully on the table.

Are you sure you don't want something to eat?

SIMON. I'm not hungry.

KRISTIN. We can't warm it up I'm afraid but you could eat it cold.

SIMON. I said I'm not hungry.

KRISTIN. Let me know if you change your mind.

She opens up a bottle of disinfectant and dabs a little of it onto a piece of cotton wool.

The evening didn't go quite as we expected.

SIMON. I heard.

KRISTIN. We had a heated discussion.

SIMON. Claire said.

KRISTIN. On various subjects.

SIMON. Okay.

KRISTIN. But if there was one overriding theme I suppose it would be priorities.

SIMON. Priorities.

KRISTIN. What's important. The things that count.

SIMON. I see.

KRISTIN. The choices that define us.

SIMON. That's interesting.

She begins to dab the disinfectant onto his palm.

KRISTIN. We'll put this disinfectant on it and then I'll use the tweezers to get the glass out.

SIMON. Thank you.

KRISTIN. But it doesn't need stitches.

Pause.

The thing about Claire and me is that we're very different kinds of people.

SIMON. Are you?

KRISTIN. We don't always see eye to eye.

SIMON. No.

KRISTIN. So it's inevitable that there'll be a little friction between us, isn't it?

A pause as she continues to apply the disinfectant to his open palm.

How are the two of you?

SIMON. How are we?

KRISTIN. I imagine it will be harder now that you're not working.

SIMON. Will it?

KRISTIN. Money, for a start.

SIMON. I see.

KRISTIN. Until you feel better. Until you feel ready again.

SIMON. Money?

KRISTIN. Until you feel you're strong enough.

SIMON. Strong enough?

KRISTIN. To go back to work I mean.

SIMON. Oh.

KRISTIN. But that money, or rather lack of it, shouldn't be a reason –

SIMON. What?

KRISTIN. For you to feel trapped in any way.

SIMON. Trapped?

Pause.

KRISTIN. I suppose what I'm saying is that I can lend you money. As much of it as you need.

SIMON. Okay.

KRISTIN. *Give* you money. And then when – *if* – you ever feel you can afford to pay me back, well then you can.

SIMON. I see.

KRISTIN. But that I wouldn't be expecting it is what I'm saying.

SIMON. Thank you.

KRISTIN *puts down the disinfectant and picks up a pair of tweezers.*

KRISTIN. Keep it still. Some of them are tiny. Tiny shards.

She starts to take out the splinters of glass one by one. She does this with great care, fastidiously.

And if you ever needed to get away. I mean for a few days, or even longer you know you can always come here. If you need some sort of break, a little distance. You know there's always a room for you here.

SIMON. A room, yes.

Pause.

KRISTIN. I know you wanted to talk to me. And I want you to know that there is nothing you can't say.

SIMON. Good.

KRISTIN. However uncomfortable.

Pause.

I want us to be friends.

SIMON. Do you?

Pause.

KRISTIN. Your brother is very worried about you. But I think he's got the wrong end of the stick.

SIMON. Has he?

Pause. She is trying to tread carefully.

KRISTIN. How do you think Claire is coping?

SIMON. How do I think Claire is coping?

KRISTIN. It must be difficult for her.

SIMON. I'm sure.

KRISTIN. She must feel inadequate at times.

SIMON. Perhaps.

KRISTIN. What I mean is that when someone close to you is suffering you must often carry the burden of it.

SIMON. Must you?

KRISTIN. And that can be an isolating place for you to find yourself in.

SIMON. I expect so.

KRISTIN. Lonely.

SIMON. Yes.

KRISTIN. And that can't be easy.

SIMON. I'm sure.

Pause.

KRISTIN. But you're coping all right. The two of you I mean. As a couple.

SIMON. A couple?

KRISTIN. Because if there's anything you want to talk to me about I want you to know that you can.

SIMON. You've said that already.

KRISTIN. However personal.

She waits for something but nothing comes. She continues to take the splinters out of his palm.

Try and keep it still, darling.

Pause.

She said you went missing last week.

SIMON. Yes.

KRISTIN. For three days. She said you went missing for three days and that when you returned you never told her where you'd been.

SIMON. No.

Again she waits, again he gives her nothing.

KRISTIN. What did you make of your brother's new girlfriend?

SIMON. Her name is Trudi.

KRISTIN. What did you make of Trudi?

SIMON. She seems nice enough.

KRISTIN. I can't say I'm not surprised.

SIMON. Surprised?

KRISTIN. She's the kind of person I ran away from America to escape from. Oh, don't get me wrong, she's nice enough...

SIMON. She is.

KRISTIN. But you know she's a Christian.

SIMON. Is she?

KRISTIN. Evangelical, that sort of thing I imagine.

SIMON. So?

KRISTIN. They met at a prayer meeting. They shared coffee and biscuits.

SIMON. That's nice.

KRISTIN. I'm just a little bewildered, that's all.

SIMON. Are you?

KRISTIN. Just a little.

SIMON. I'm not.

Pause.

I woke up one morning and realised that pretty much everything we are and everything we do is a response against you. So, no, I'm not bewildered in the least.

KRISTIN *continues as if she didn't hear this.*

KRISTIN. But she's nice enough, I suppose. And he seems to like her which is the most important thing.

SIMON. It is.

Pause. She looks closely at his palm.

KRISTIN. We have to make sure they're all out otherwise it could get infected. And then we can go to sleep. You look tired.

SIMON. I'm not.

KRISTIN. I am.

SIMON. I came to talk to you.

She continues taking out the splinters.

KRISTIN. Your brother had a go at me for not mentioning you in the book. He didn't understand that the book was about the work, more about my professional life and less about the personal things. He seemed offended in some way and implied that you were as well. I suppose I ought to apologise if it wasn't clear enough. I certainly didn't set out to upset you.

SIMON. No.

KRISTIN. So that's that.

SIMON. Yes. That's that.

KRISTIN. I was thinking in the morning we should go for a walk. At least to the foot of the hills and maybe even halfway up them. The weather will be good, it said.

SIMON. All right.

KRISTIN. And we could all do with the exercise.

SIMON. We could.

KRISTIN. Fresh air.

SIMON. Yes.

KRISTIN. The oxygen.

Pause.

SIMON. Lately I've been doing some retracing.

KRISTIN. Retracing?

SIMON. Locating the moments, finding the locations, remembering, and then suddenly going, 'Ah! So this is where it was. This is the place, that was the time when I first said to myself: "This is who I am, how it is, what I'm worth."'

KRISTIN. What you're worth?

SIMON. This is where I was shaped. This is where the music started.

KRISTIN. What music?

SIMON. This is the moment that set the soundtrack for the rest of my life. Finding those moments. That's what I mean by retracing.

Pause. She puts down his hand and the tweezers.

KRISTIN. I need to talk to you about something.

SIMON. Because the thing is I've always felt this way.

KRISTIN. What way?

SIMON. Disjointed.

KRISTIN. Disjointed?

SIMON. And dislocated. Disillusioned. Dis-this, dis-that. Disturbed, distracted, discombobulated.

KRISTIN. I don't understand what you mean.

SIMON. But you keep going. You shrug it off. You say to yourself, 'This is the way it is for everyone.' And then one day you realise that it isn't. That your complete incapacity to feel any sort of self-worth is your own personal brand of misery.

KRISTIN. I don't understand you.

SIMON. So you keep going until that day. And then suddenly you run out of fuel. You can't lie to yourself any more. You've always felt that way. And so it catches up with you, that's all.

Pause.

KRISTIN. There's something you need to know.

SIMON. So that's why I came. To tell you about my retracing. And to ask you a question or two.

KRISTIN. It isn't easy but I've decided that it's the right thing.

SIMON. What is?

KRISTIN. I need to talk to you about Claire.

SIMON. What about her.

KRISTIN. I wasn't going to. I didn't want to.

SIMON. What about Claire?

KRISTIN. But I think I have to. Talk to you.

SIMON. About what?

KRISTIN. About something that happened this evening.

SIMON. I see.

KRISTIN. Because maybe knowing things for what they are is important now.

SIMON. That isn't why I came.

KRISTIN. So maybe it's for the best.

SIMON. Not to talk about Claire.

Pause.

KRISTIN. Her phone rang earlier. I thought it was mine. I answered it. Something embarrassing happened.

SIMON. I don't want to talk about Claire.

KRISTIN. I answered it by mistake. Thinking it was mine.

SIMON. That's not why I came here.

KRISTIN. So I answered it.

SIMON. SO PLEASE LET'S NOT TALK ABOUT CLAIRE!

Pause. She returns her attention to his hand.

KRISTIN. We're nearly finished. And then we'll put a plaster on it. There's only a couple more.

SIMON. Lately I can't stop thinking of that year.

KRISTIN. What year?

SIMON. The year you took us to Florence.

KRISTIN. What about it?

SIMON. After the divorce. You were working on your book.

KRISTIN. The first one.

SIMON. And you took us with you.

KRISTIN. I did.

Pause.

SIMON. Do you remember the house?

KRISTIN. Of course I do.

SIMON. Overlooking the city.

KRISTIN. That view.

SIMON. There was an orange tree in the garden.

KRISTIN. I remember.

SIMON. It was vast.

KRISTIN. We used to sit in its shade. In the afternoons. The three of us. I'd be traipsing around churches in the mornings doing my research. Then I'd pick you up from that funny school and then we'd spend the afternoons in the shade of that vast orange tree. I'd be ploughing through those heavy tomes and making notes for the book and you and your brother would be doing your homework.

SIMON. Do you remember?

KRISTIN. How could I forget?

SIMON. I've been thinking about it a lot.

KRISTIN. It was the happiest year of my life. Me and my boys.

SIMON. Sometimes on Sundays you'd take us with you. To the basilicas, the galleries. Or we'd get in the car and drive to some other town. You were always working. I remember

spending hours in the back of some church somewhere
watching you scribbling notes with your head tilted back
staring up at some fucking fresco.

KRISTIN. I was obsessed, it's true.

SIMON. I always felt I was competing for your attention.

KRISTIN. I suppose it was a vocation. A calling.

SIMON. Yes.

KRISTIN. But I took you with me. I took you to Florence with me.

SIMON. I know.

KRISTIN. And then he took you away.

Pause.

SIMON. We always thought you'd follow us.

KRISTIN. I'm sure.

SIMON. We thought you'd come for us.

KRISTIN. I know you did.

SIMON. Fight for us.

KRISTIN. Yes.

SIMON. Because that's what we thought parents did.

KRISTIN. Of course.

SIMON. Mothers.

KRISTIN. Of course you did.

SIMON. So we waited, and waited.

KRISTIN. Yes.

SIMON. And waited.

KRISTIN. I know.

SIMON. But you never came.

Pause.

I was seven years old.

KRISTIN. I know how old you were.

Pause. She takes out a plaster and starts to apply it to his hand.

They're all out. We'll just put a plaster on it and then we're done.

SIMON. I mean if your parent dies when you're that age, then obviously you feel something, I don't know, irreparable, long-lasting, something you never quite get over.

KRISTIN. Of course you do.

SIMON. A loss, an injury, something that never quite mends.

KRISTIN. Yes.

SIMON. But when a parent, when your mother –

KRISTIN. I know what you're going to say.

SIMON. Doesn't come for you it's just as damaging.

KRISTIN. Of course it is.

SIMON. Abandons you, it's just as harmful.

KRISTIN. I didn't abandon you.

SIMON. And maybe even worse.

KRISTIN. He took you away.

SIMON. But you never came. And then you became this person we'd spend holidays with.

Pause. She starts to pack away the first-aid kit.

Do you remember once I came to Italy on my own? It was the summer. I must have been – what – thirteen? Peter had gone to stay with a friend in Cornwall. Dad put me on the train in London. You were supposed to pick me up in Genoa.

KRISTIN. I can't remember.

SIMON. But something happened and you never made it. I mean you did eventually but it was like a day later.

KRISTIN. I really can't remember.

SIMON. But I'd been on my own through the night. I had a phone number for you in Italy but I rang it and there wasn't an answer. I remember all the trains had come in and all the people had been greeted by their families or friends and I sat there watching them and waiting to spot your face in the crowd.

KRISTIN. Why are you telling me this now?

SIMON. But it got dark and you never came. The station emptied and these two women came out and started mopping the platforms. I remember that.

KRISTIN. Why are you telling me this?

SIMON. It must have been one in the morning and I was lying on this bench when this man approached me.

KRISTIN. A man?

SIMON. There was a café on the side of the platform and I think he'd been sitting there for quite a long time and had noticed this boy in a suit looking rather lost. So he came to talk to me.

KRISTIN. I think I do remember now.

SIMON. Remember?

KRISTIN. There'd been a misunderstanding. Crossed wires. Your father had said –

SIMON. It doesn't really matter.

KRISTIN. He'd left a message with the cleaning lady who came in once a week. Which was a stupid thing to do as she didn't speak a word of English and his Italian was non-existent. Anyway, she got it wrong. Or wrote it down on a piece of paper which I didn't find until it was too late. But that's what caused it all. It was a stupid thing to do. And I'd been working. I remember there was a lecture that I –

SIMON. He must have been – I don't know about forty, or something. Probably had bad acne when he was younger because his skin was slightly pockmarked.

KRISTIN. But that's what happened. Your father had been careless.

SIMON. He spoke quite good English but I think he was German or Dutch or something. Doesn't really matter though does it, what nationality he was. Anyway he asked me if I was all right –

KRISTIN. Why are you telling me this now?

SIMON. And I said that I was and that I was waiting for my mother but that she would be there soon and that I would wait for her until she got there.

KRISTIN. Why are you telling me this?

SIMON. He then said that he was worried about a boy of my age spending the whole night on my own and asked me if I wanted to have a Coke with him in the cafeteria. I said why not so we went to the cafeteria but it had just closed and there was nowhere else to go.

KRISTIN. So did he leave you alone?

SIMON. I remember then we sat down on a bench outside the cafeteria and we talked and at one point he said something like, 'If I was your parent I would never leave you waiting for me on a station platform all night long.' This made an impression on me because half of me was angry at him for saying it and I wanted to defend you and explain to him that it was all a misunderstanding, that you would show up and everything would be all right and half of me agreed with him and was happy that he'd expressed it in that particular way.

KRISTIN. What a strange thing to say.

SIMON. And then he said, 'Why don't you come back to my house and have something to eat and you can rest and then I'll bring you back in the morning.'

KRISTIN. What happened?

SIMON. And even though I felt, no I *knew* that it was dangerous, that it was wrong for me to follow this man back to his house I stood up and picked up my bag and followed him.

KRISTIN. You went to his house?

SIMON. And part of me was thinking – 'This will show her, this will show her, this will fucking show her.'

KRISTIN. You went to this man's house?

SIMON. So we walked through the streets of Genoa and it was in the middle of the night and there was nobody about. I remember thinking that we must be very near the sea because there many seagulls in the sky.

KRISTIN. Seagulls?

SIMON. Then eventually we got to this old building and he opened the door and we walked up these stairs that stank of urine or something. His flat was at the top and he opened the door and let me in. He asked me to sit down and then he gave me a glass of wine and made some joke about not telling my parents.

KRISTIN. What happened?

SIMON. And then he cooked a meal. I watched him taking things out of a cupboard and out of the fridge and he started preparing a meal. He made pasta with a tomato sauce and as he cooked he talked to me about what had brought him to Italy and about other things too and I noticed that he was nervous and that his hands were shaking a little and I could feel the wine whooshing around in my head.

KRISTIN. Did he hurt you?

SIMON. At one point I asked him if I could use the bathroom so he took me down the hall and showed me where it was and I went in and closed the door behind me. I remember the light in the bathroom was very weak as if the bulb was broken or something, it was quite dark. So that when I looked into the mirror I could only just see my face. I stood there for some time just staring at myself and wondering why you hadn't shown up at the station.

KRISTIN. Why have you never told me all this before?

SIMON. And it was when I was trying to see my face in the mirror that I heard him breathing outside the door. So he'd been standing there all along, on the other side of the door. And then I tried to open it, to open the door but it was jammed.

KRISTIN. Jammed?

SIMON. As if it was blocked. As if he was blocking it from the
other side.

KRISTIN. What did he do to you? What did this man do to you?

SIMON. Then after a little it opened and he wasn't there. He was
back in the kitchen. So I went back. I wanted to run away but I
was too scared.

KRISTIN. Did he hurt you?

SIMON. The food was ready so we ate in silence. After we'd
eaten we sat on the sofa for some time and he kept talking
nervously and then he asked me if I wanted to sleep in his bed
with him and I said that I didn't. Then he took some sheets out
of a cupboard and turned the sofa into a bed for me and then
he said he'd wake me at six in the morning and walk me back
to the station. And that's what he did. He walked me back to
the bench that he'd found me on.

KRISTIN. So he never hurt you?

SIMON. Lately I can't seem to get that night out of my head. I
keep thinking of myself trying to find my face in the mirror in
the dim-lit bathroom of that dark building in that strange and
foreign city.

Pause.

Where were you?

KRISTIN. I told you. Your father had made a mistake and had –

SIMON. No. I mean, where were you? Where were you? Where
were you?

Pause.

You were never there. I have to tell you now that the thing I
remember most about you is your absence. I have to be honest
and tell you that. That's what I wanted to tell you when I read
your book. That's my response to it.

Pause.

So you look for those moments. And you say to yourself,
'That's when it was.'

Pause. KRISTIN *stands and picks up the first-aid kit. She walks over to the counter and puts it back into the cupboard.*

KRISTIN. I'm very tired. We can continue talking tomorrow.

I've left a towel at the end of the bed if you want to have a shower in the morning.

SIMON. I saw it.

KRISTIN *walks over to him and kisses him on the forehead.*

KRISTIN. Goodnight.

SIMON. I know about Claire. What it was you wanted to tell me. Do you blame her? I haven't been around for some time now. In any way.

Pause.

KRISTIN *leaves the room.* SIMON *leans over and picks up the framed photograph that* HUGH *gave* KRISTIN *as a gift.*

He looks at it closely, as if trying to understand something about it.

Lights fade to darkness.

Scene Two

The next morning. HUGH, TRUDI *and* CLAIRE *are in the kitchen. They are having breakfast –* TRUDI *is eating a bowl of cereal and* CLAIRE *is playing with a piece of toast.* HUGH *is drinking coffee and casually leafing through the newspaper.*

CLAIRE. All I'm really saying is that I think you're very lucky.

TRUDI. I am?

CLAIRE. To have your faith I mean.

TRUDI. Okay.

CLAIRE. Especially nowadays.

TRUDI. How do you mean?

CLAIRE. Although it seems religion is making a major comeback.

HUGH. Is it?

CLAIRE. People looking for some sort of certainty.

HUGH. I see.

CLAIRE. In times of turmoil.

HUGH. All of a sudden dictators, biblical or otherwise, seem rather alluring.

CLAIRE. It's inevitable.

HUGH. Anyone who promises they can sort things out for you in one way or another.

TRUDI. Maybe.

HUGH. And maybe punish the suspected perpetrators.

TRUDI. Okay.

HUGH. Another example of human nature in all its shimmering intelligence.

Pause.

CLAIRE. I do like Jesus though.

TRUDI. Like him?

HUGH. How do you mean, you like him?

CLAIRE. Well, what I mean is –

HUGH. He's not a brand of toothpaste for fuck's sake –

CLAIRE. That everything he stands for kind of makes sense –

HUGH. Or a pasta sauce.

TRUDI. Does it?

CLAIRE. I mean like everything he says in the sermon on the mountain –

HUGH. What mountain?

CLAIRE. Kind of resonates with me.

TRUDI. Okay.

CLAIRE. Love thy neighbour and all that.

HUGH. Yes, that's a good one.

CLAIRE. To err is human, to forgive divine.

TRUDI. I don't know if –

HUGH. I think that was Oscar Wilde.

CLAIRE. So I completely understand why you would want to make it such an integral part of your life.

TRUDI. It's not really –

CLAIRE. I did get drawn to Buddhism for a time.

HUGH. Oh?

CLAIRE. The chanting really stills you.

TRUDI. Does it?

CLAIRE. And I suppose if Christianity still held on to its more mystical side –

HUGH. I know what you mean.

CLAIRE. I might be more drawn to it.

HUGH. Might you?

CLAIRE. The Orthodox Church still has some of that.

HUGH. It's very dramatic.

CLAIRE. Incense, candles, chandeliers.

HUGH. Those funny hats.

CLAIRE. It kind of draws you in.

HUGH. English vicars don't quite have the same allure.

CLAIRE. But religion generally gives me the creeps. Especially the more fundamental Muslims. The *anger*.

Pause.

TRUDI. The thing is...

CLAIRE. Yes?

TRUDI. I don't want to be rude but –

CLAIRE. Rude?

TRUDI. I mean the way you talk about it, I mean about religion, I don't really understand you. I mean I think Hugh is right to point out that it's not a product. It's much more than that.

CLAIRE. I wasn't –

TRUDI. It's like, I'm sorry but the way you were talking about it just now, about Christianity and Buddhism and the Orthodox Church you make them all sound like items on a shopping list for you to choose from, but for most people –

CLAIRE. I'm sorry, I didn't mean to offend you.

TRUDI. For most people it's probably not like that. The thing is for many people it might be less of a luxury item and more like the *only* thing they have – a lifeline, a reason to continue, their only hope – so to trivialise it is not necessarily helpful and I know a lot of the times when you see those men –

HUGH. What men?

TRUDI. Those men, in Pakistan or wherever screaming and shouting they seem I don't know, crazy, or mad or completely *medieval* or something – well I know that when you see these things it's easy I suppose to laugh at it or be appalled by it or condemn it as some sort of ancient superstition but the point is – the thing to understand is – that maybe some of us had an opportunity – *have* an opportunity, I don't know if it's too late – to offer some sort of alternative but because we were greedy, or selfish or just plain stupid we've wasted it. And that is really quite sad.

CLAIRE. I didn't really mean –

PETER *has entered the room. He stands by the door, slightly surprised by* TRUDI's *tone of voice.*

TRUDI. I mean we have been so privileged, I'm sure people will look back at us in five hundred years from now and be amazed at just how rich we were and they'll ask what we did, I mean what the legacy of all that phenomenal wealth was but when they, I don't know, excavate or whatever, all they'll find is a few infinity pools and a whole lot of expensive clothes.

CLAIRE. The thing I was trying –

TRUDI. And if you really don't have clean drinking water and a little education I'm sure waving a banner and frothing at the mouth seems like a reasonable option.

HUGH. Hear, hear.

CLAIRE. I don't think I was –

TRUDI. I'm sorry but I really felt like I needed to say that.

PETER catches her eye and there is a look between them.

He looks a little worried – as if there is something of KRISTIN growing in her.

PETER. Are you feeling okay?

TRUDI. I'm fine.

PETER. I can't find my toothbrush.

TRUDI. I put it in the bag.

PETER. It isn't in there, I checked.

TRUDI. I'm sure I put it in the bag.

PETER. I couldn't see it.

TRUDI. I'll find it for you.

They leave the room just as KRISTIN is entering.

KRISTIN. Good morning.

HUGH. Hello, darling.

TRUDI. Hi, Kristin.

CLAIRE. Hello.

PETER. Hi.

HUGH. The coffee's hot.

PETER and TRUDI exit.

KRISTIN. Is Simon still in bed?

CLAIRE. No, he's gone.

KRISTIN. Gone?

CLAIRE. He left at seven.

HUGH. None of us got to say goodbye.

KRISTIN. How do you mean, he's gone?

CLAIRE. He'll be home by now.

KRISTIN. I thought he'd stay for breakfast.

CLAIRE. He didn't sleep much.

KRISTIN. I thought I'd see him.

CLAIRE. And then I woke up and he was gone.

KRISTIN. I see.

Pause. HUGH *senses that he should leave the two women alone. He checks his pockets.*

HUGH. I've left my bloody car keys on the bedside table.

He leaves the room. There is a pause as KRISTIN *goes to the cafetière and pours herself a cup of coffee.*

KRISTIN. I'm surprised you're still here.

CLAIRE. Are you?

KRISTIN. Just a little.

CLAIRE. I'm not in make-up till eleven.

Pause.

Besides I wanted to talk to you.

KRISTIN. What about?

CLAIRE. I don't think I'll be seeing you again.

KRISTIN. Oh?

CLAIRE. So I thought it only right to say goodbye. Consider it a mark of respect.

Pause.

I don't know what you and Simon talked about last night. But when he came back to the room he woke me up and we chatted till dawn. You'll be happy to hear we've decided to part ways.

KRISTIN. Have you indeed?

CLAIRE. It was inevitable. We've just been putting it off, that's all. I'm surprised we lasted for a year and a half.

KRISTIN. So am I.

CLAIRE. He said he realised the only reason he was attracted to me was because I was the polar opposite of you.

KRISTIN. I'm sure he meant it as a compliment.

CLAIRE. I'm sure he did.

Pause. KRISTIN *puts down her coffee and starts to busy herself around the kitchen – she gets a dishcloth from the sink and starts to wipe down the kitchen table.*

It's funny. When you said last night that you thought I was good in *A Doll's House* my heart missed a beat. I nearly leapt for joy. How do you do that?

KRISTIN. I really wouldn't know.

CLAIRE. Did I ever tell you about my father?

KRISTIN. What about him?

CLAIRE. I watched him slowly drown in a mountain of unpaid bills. When I was thirteen he was declared bankrupt. I used to come home every day after school and the bathroom door was always closed and the sound was always the same – the sound of my mother's stifled sobs. Then she'd come out with a smile on her face and cook dinner. One day, he left and never came back. My mother and I moved to a small rented flat and lived on benefits. The first day I moved my bed and there was a whole lot of blood on the wall. I spent all my time in that flat wondering what had happened before we arrived. I came up with quite a few upsetting scenarios. I had a vivid imagination.

Pause.

Since then most of my life I've been running away from
unpaid bills, stifled sobs and those dark-red stains. That may
have affected some of my artistic choices.

Pause.

That's my individual story. But something tells me that
somewhere along the line you've stopped listening to people's
individual stories. I wonder when that happened.

Pause. She waits for something from KRISTIN *but nothing
comes.*

There's a part of me that admires you. The way you've held on
to the things you've believed in. But your idealism has turned
into hardness, Kristin. It has a thick, thick shell. *You* do. A
carapace. Isn't that the word?

Again, KRISTIN *doesn't reply.*

Why does she demonise me like that? I kept asking myself.
Why does she vilify me? Why does she scrutinise everything I
do and then condemn it without a second thought?

KRISTIN. Is that what I do?

CLAIRE. And then I decided it's got nothing to do with me
really. It's not about me.

KRISTIN. Isn't it?

CLAIRE. It's about you, Kristin.

KRISTIN. Oh?

CLAIRE. When I was in my room last night I had a little bit of a
revelation.

KRISTIN. That must have been a novel experience.

CLAIRE. They say don't they that when people get older they
just become worse versions of themselves.

KRISTIN. Is that what they say?

CLAIRE. Maybe in some people that's a little more pronounced.

KRISTIN. Maybe.

CLAIRE. And I expect it's really a case of having to hold on to everything you are. Everything you *were*. The choices you made, the paths you followed. Because if you start to question them, if you start to doubt them... well then you're fucked really, aren't you?

KRISTIN. I wouldn't know.

CLAIRE. So you hang on with every fibre of your being.

Pause.

It must be exhausting being you.

KRISTIN. Thank you for that searing insight but I'd stick to the acting if I were you.

TRUDI *and* PETER *return, followed by* HUGH.

TRUDI. It was in the bag of course.

KRISTIN. Have you all had breakfast?

TRUDI. I have toast.

HUGH. I called the electrician. He'll be here by noon.

KRISTIN. Thank you.

PETER. Sweetie, do you want some more coffee?

TRUDI. Thanks, honey.

PETER *fills up their cups.*

CLAIRE. I really ought to be making a move.

KRISTIN. Drive carefully.

PETER. We should get going soon too.

TRUDI. Your flight is at two.

KRISTIN. Where are you off to this time?

PETER. Botswana.

HUGH. You really do go to the most extraordinary places.

PETER. Yes.

HUGH. You global adventurer.

TRUDI. And you haven't even packed yet.

CLAIRE. Bye, Peter.

She kisses PETER *on the cheek.*

PETER. Bye. I'm sorry that –

CLAIRE. It's fine.

PETER. But I hope we see you again.

CLAIRE. Maybe.

TRUDI. We'll look out for the...

CLAIRE. Weeknights at seven. On Sky.

TRUDI. I look forward to it.

CLAIRE. Trudi.

TRUDI. It was great to meet you. And I apologise if I sounded a little defensive just now –

CLAIRE. It's fine.

TRUDI. But I felt at that particular moment that I needed to say what was on my mind.

CLAIRE. As I said, you're very lucky to have something to believe in.

TRUDI. And I'm sorry about your Japanese dress.

CLAIRE *walks up to* KRISTIN.

CLAIRE. Kristin.

KRISTIN. Claire.

CLAIRE. Don't forget to eat the mango meringue.

CLAIRE *gives* KRISTIN *an unexpected kiss on the cheek.* KRISTIN *is slightly taken aback by it.*

KRISTIN. Take care.

CLAIRE. It's been challenging.

TRUDI. Bye, Claire.

HUGH. Cheerio.

CLAIRE. Bye.

She leaves.

HUGH. Enjoy Thursday.

Pause.

Right. I have some urgent gardening to attend to.

KRISTIN. Don't want to neglect your turnips.

HUGH. Certainly not.

A slight pause.

TRUDI. Before you go, Hugh, I... Sweetie?

She looks at PETER *but he doesn't pick up.*

The thing is that when we came here last night we were expecting... well, we had something that we wanted to share with you –

PETER. Oh.

TRUDI. Something that we wished, something that we *hoped* would make you very happy.

HUGH. I'm riveted.

TRUDI. But then the evening took an unexpected turn.

HUGH. Did it?

TRUDI. And it just didn't seem appropriate at the time to...

PETER. To tell you.

HUGH. The suspense is killing me.

TRUDI. But now, this morning, I don't see why we shouldn't so the thing we wanted to tell you is –

PETER. Sweetie.

TRUDI. Is that we're engaged. To be married. To each other.

Pause.

HUGH. How glorious.

TRUDI. Of course I didn't really envision telling you like this.

PETER. No.

TRUDI. I had imagined that after dinner, maybe after you'd
blown out the candles on your cake –

HUGH. That fucking mango thing.

TRUDI. And we were all sitting around the table, all together,
that Peter and I, well one of us at least would stand up and sort
of announce it and then we'd have some more champagne.
That's how I imagined it.

KRISTIN. Things rarely turn out the way we expected.

TRUDI. I'm beginning to see that.

PETER. Anyway, it's true, we're getting married.

KRISTIN (*checking the fridge*). I'm afraid we're all out of
champagne.

HUGH. Must have been all that marvellous celebrating we did
last night.

KRISTIN. But congratulations.

TRUDI. Thank you.

KRISTIN. Really, congratulations.

HUGH. Have you got a date?

PETER. A date?

HUGH. For the big day.

TRUDI. May next year.

HUGH. A spring wedding.

TRUDI. And then a honeymoon in Egypt and the Holy Land.

HUGH. Interesting choice.

TRUDI. It's just that I've always wanted to see that part of the
world.

PETER. Me too.

KRISTIN. You've never told me that.

PETER. I don't tell you everything.

HUGH. Israel?

TRUDI. Sure. Jerusalem. Bethlehem. Just to see really, what it's like.

KRISTIN. A pilgrimage of sorts.

TRUDI. If you want to call it that. It's just I'm not really a beach person.

KRISTIN. No.

TRUDI. So I prefer trips that have a cultural relevance. Historical, that kind of thing.

KRISTIN. Religious.

TRUDI. I promise I won't have Peter baptised in the River Jordan.

KRISTIN. That's a relief.

TRUDI. Just to see where it all started.

KRISTIN. Why don't you do Greece? Athens, Delphi, the Peloponnese.

HUGH. Even their choice of honeymoon is a threat to her.

KRISTIN. The Greek islands are beautiful in May.

She walks over to PETER *and kisses him on the cheek.*

But congratulations.

Pause. With some hesitation and awkwardness she also kisses TRUDI *on the cheek.*

TRUDI. Kristin, can I ask you a favour?

KRISTIN. What is it?

TRUDI. You know how much I love your house. I mean the way you've decorated it. And Peter was saying the other day that the most beautiful room in the house is your study. The room you work in.

KRISTIN. I'm listening.

TRUDI. And I was just wondering if before we leave I could just look at it. Stick my head in the door kind of thing. But I realise that you may not want me to. That it's private, sacred to you. So if you don't want me to that's fine. I'll understand.

KRISTIN. Why wouldn't I want you to?

TRUDI. I'll completely understand.

KRISTIN. It's not private, at least not when I'm not in there working and it's certainly not sacred. I'm not a priest.

TRUDI. Thank you. I'll just stick my head in the door.

KRISTIN. I'll show it to you.

TRUDI. Thank you.

KRISTIN. Oh and we might as well pick up that book I was telling you about. The one on African tribal art. It's to the right of my desk somewhere, in a pile. We'll have a look at it and see if I can find anything.

TRUDI. Sure.

KRISTIN. We'll be back in a minute.

HUGH. And then I really must move my skinny arse.

KRISTIN *and* TRUDI *leave the room.* HUGH *has returned to perusing the newspaper.*

PETER. Anything interesting?

HUGH. Just the usual. Famine, war and celebrity facelifts.

PETER. Nice.

HUGH. What an enlightened species we are.

Pause.

Call me a witness for the defence.

PETER. Sorry?

HUGH. I think it's time for my testimony.

PETER. What testimony?

HUGH. I was there. I saw. I heard. I know.

PETER. Know what?

HUGH. I'm not saying you don't have an argument, I'm not saying that you – and Simon, God bless him – haven't paid a price, haven't a right to recriminate, to attack, to feel all those tangled, seething feelings that you do. But I was there.

PETER. What are you talking about?

HUGH. And last night, when you went for her jugular I wanted to go for yours. Even though I was trying to hold down a very disagreeable serving of beef in oyster sauce.

PETER. So?

HUGH. So, I'm the peacemaker. I'm also rather English. I'd rather have a limb amputated than make a scene. But last night I wanted to go for you, boy.

PETER. I was provoked.

HUGH. Oh, I know, she is to moderation and diplomacy what I am to heterosexuality – she just doesn't do it.

PETER. She doesn't.

HUGH. But I still wanted to grab you by the neck and say, 'I was there. I'm a witness.'

Pause.

You may joke about Gauloises cigarettes but you didn't know her back then. Before it all went so terribly wrong. I don't know about the others. Those men and women who were also there, doing what we were doing. Marching in our sandals, as Claire put it. And maybe she's right, maybe all they really wanted was to move to big houses in suburbs. But there was something in your mother's eyes that was genuine.

PETER. Genuine?

HUGH. She was extraordinary. *Visionary* is the word.

PETER. Okay.

HUGH. The thing you really need to know is that I can put my hand on my heart and say to you that in those eyes I saw that she thought – naively, maybe, who knows – that she was doing it all for you.

PETER. Is that what you saw?

HUGH. But then you'd need to believe that people like that actually exist. People who care in that particular way. And maybe you don't any more.

PETER. I don't understand what you –

HUGH. Chew on that a little while, you ingrate.

KRISTIN *and* TRUDI *return.* KRISTIN *is holding a large book on African art.*

TRUDI. That is such a beautiful room, Kristin.

KRISTIN. I'm glad you like it.

TRUDI. It's atmospheric and so cosy.

KRISTIN. Thank you.

KRISTIN *sits at the table, opens the book and starts to scour the index.*

Right, what country did you say it was from?

PETER. Liberia.

TRUDI. And all those books. Books, books, books. Books everywhere.

KRISTIN. Yes.

TRUDI. I've never seen so many books in my life.

KRISTIN. Haven't you?

TRUDI. And the view. The way you've positioned the desk. To sit there, looking out over the fields and the hills thinking of what you're going to write next.

KRISTIN. I won't be writing anything for some time. Here we go, Liberia. Masks.

HUGH. I'm off.

TRUDI. It's been really wonderful to meet you, Hugh.

HUGH. Likewise. You really are a rather adorable creature.

TRUDI. Thank you.

HUGH. And I'm very happy that you're planning to teach this man a little sense. Religious or not is not really the point. You're a sensible girl, I can tell.

KRISTIN. I'll call you this evening.

HUGH. Do. And I'll see you on Saturday.

KRISTIN. You will.

HUGH. I'll pick you up and then we'll take the train. We need to be in London by eleven at the latest so I'll be here eight thirty-ish.

KRISTIN. Good.

TRUDI. What's happening on Saturday?

HUGH. A pro-Kurdish march.

PETER. Naturally.

HUGH. So I'll see you then.

KRISTIN. I'll be ready.

He kisses her.

HUGH. We never ate that fucking cake.

KRISTIN. No.

HUGH. Have it for lunch.

KRISTIN. Or we could have some now.

TRUDI. I'm okay thanks, Kristin.

PETER. Me too.

HUGH *kisses* TRUDI.

HUGH. Look after the brute.

TRUDI. I'll try.

HUGH. Have fun in Burundi.

PETER. Botswana.

HUGH. Try not to exploit the locals too horribly.

KRISTIN. It's his job.

PETER. Goodbye, Hugh.

HUGH. Goodbye.

He moves towards the door then stops and turns to look at PETER.

Remember what I said about the eyes.

KRISTIN. What eyes?

HUGH *leaves*.

PETER. I just need to use the bathroom. And I'll get the bag.

TRUDI. Sure.

PETER *leaves the room. There is a pause.* KRISTIN *continues to look through the book.*

It's funny.

KRISTIN. What is?

TRUDI. When we were in your study I happened to glance up at your bookshelves and I let my eyes scan all the titles, you know, the spines of the books and... can I ask you something?

KRISTIN. You may.

TRUDI. Is it just my imagination or have you... what I'm asking is have your books been ordered chronologically? Have you ordered them chronologically?

KRISTIN. I have.

TRUDI. Why have you done that?

KRISTIN. At heart I'm an optimist.

TRUDI. An optimist?

KRISTIN. I like to believe that we're evolving in some way.

TRUDI. Anyway, I noticed. I started at one side and there were lots of names and many of them were women. And then slowly there were fewer and fewer of them. Women I mean. And I think it was only like the nineteen fifties. And by the end of the second shelf it was all men. And poor George Eliot, all on her own.

KRISTIN. Yes.

TRUDI. I mean you forget how recent it is.

KRISTIN. Do you?

TRUDI. I suppose what I'm saying is that something happened in the sixties, the seventies. All those women's voices.

KRISTIN. Yes.

TRUDI. I mean we all know that we've been living in a patriarchal world, in a masculine... what's the word?

KRISTIN. Ordering?

TRUDI. Ordering of the world, that's right. They've made a bit of a... what's that expression that Peter's always using... a dog's dinner?

KRISTIN. Yes, that's a good expression.

TRUDI. They've made a bit of a dog's dinner of it on their own, haven't they?

KRISTIN. You could say that.

TRUDI. But that something happened in the sixties, the seventies, that had never happened before. And if there was one thing worth fighting for, one thing worth holding on to it was that. So thank you, I suppose is what I'm saying.

Pause. KRISTIN *has found what she was looking for.*

KRISTIN. Eureka. Well, it's close enough anyway.

TRUDI. What is?

KRISTIN. Wouldn't you say? I mean look, the forehead, the broadness of it, the shape.

KRISTIN *shows* TRUDI *the photograph she has found in the book.* TRUDI *picks up the mask to compare it.*

TRUDI. Oh, my God that's incredible.

KRISTIN. The similarity.

TRUDI. They're almost exactly the same.

KRISTIN. Aren't they just?

TRUDI. What does it say?

KRISTIN. Wait. Let's see.

TRUDI. How weird. They're almost identical.

KRISTIN (*reading from the book*). 'Mask from the Sande
Society, a woman's association found in Liberia, Sierra Leone
and Guinea that champions women's social and political
interests and promotes their solidarity vis-à-vis the Poro, a
complementary institution for men. The broad forehead and
long face, commonly used in masks from this region, are
associated with the sense of responsibility and duty that
accompanies the privileged position of power and influence.
The wearers of this mask would connect to the spirit of the
community in which they lived and experience the insight that
the survival and wellbeing of the individual is inexorably
interdependent with the survival and wellbeing of that very
community.'

Pause.

TRUDI. I was thinking. The pioneers. The first ones in uncharted
territory. The mapmakers. They're the ones who pay the price
so that the rest of us don't have to.

Pause.

And I know why you didn't write about them in your book.
Why you didn't even mention them.

KRISTIN. Oh?

TRUDI. Because you couldn't.

Pause.

Some things are so big, aren't they? Too big. If you had even
put pen to paper and written their names the earth would have
opened up beneath your feet. You would never have been able
to write the book. The *loss*.

She waits for KRISTIN *to respond but she doesn't.*

I know. I understand. It's only human.

PETER *returns. He is holding their overnight bag.*

PETER. Done.

KRISTIN. Are you sure you don't want another coffee for the road?

PETER. We really must be going.

TRUDI. Yes.

She realises that she needs to leave PETER *alone with* KRISTIN *for a moment.*

I have to...

PETER. You have to what?

TRUDI. I need to...

She throws him a look.

I'll only be a minute.

She leaves the room. There is a pause as PETER *and* KRISTIN *are left alone.* KRISTIN *picks up the mask which* TRUDI *has left on the table.*

PETER. The things I said last night.

KRISTIN. What about them?

PETER. Maybe I got carried away.

KRISTIN. No you didn't. You said what you've always wanted to say, and so did your brother. It's fine. I'm a big girl, I can take it.

PETER. Can you?

Pause.

KRISTIN. That day. I went to the school to pick you up and he had taken you. I ran around the streets like a madwoman. I opened your cupboards. Your clothes were gone. Your books, your toys. In one day the house seemed to change for ever. Its rooms echoed. I was alone.

Pause.

Something about me finding my voice threatened him. Oh, he was progressive. He called himself a liberal. An enlightened man in every sense of the word. Theoretically. But when the moment came he couldn't quite live up to it. So he twisted my arm, twisted *my soul* into making a choice. And I had to take a stand.

TRUDI *comes back in her coat.*

TRUDI. Okay.

PETER. Let's go.

KRISTIN. I know. Botswana.

TRUDI. I'm ready.

KRISTIN. Off you go.

TRUDI. It's been such a privilege to meet you, Kristin.

KRISTIN. I've enjoyed meeting you too.

TRUDI. It was nice to spend time with a fellow American on foreign soil.

KRISTIN. You found me.

TRUDI. I hope to see you again soon.

KRISTIN. I'm sure we'll be seeing a lot of each other.

PETER. Not if I can help it.

TRUDI. Thank you so much for everything.

KRISTIN. You're very welcome.

PETER. I'll call you when I'm back.

KRISTIN. Do that.

TRUDI. Bye, Kristin.

They open the door and are about to leave.

KRISTIN. Don't let the thugs win, Peter.

PETER. I'll do my best.

TRUDI. Bye-bye.

KRISTIN. Remember work is about offering.

PETER. Is it?

KRISTIN. Not usury.

PETER. I'll make a note of that.

PETER *leaves and* TRUDI *is about to follow him but she stays back.*

TRUDI. Kristin.

KRISTIN. Trudi?

TRUDI. One last thing.

KRISTIN. Go on.

TRUDI. That thing I said last night. About forgiveness.

KRISTIN. Oh, that.

TRUDI. I think you misunderstood me.

KRISTIN. I did?

TRUDI. I didn't mean their father. I wasn't talking about you forgiving their father.

There is a beat as TRUDI *waits to see if* KRISTIN *has understood what she means. Then, when she knows that she has she walks forward and embraces her.* KRISTIN *does not respond – it is as if she is frozen.*

TRUDI *leaves the room and* KRISTIN *does not move. She is like a pillar of stone. A few seconds pass, we hear a car driving away.* KRISTIN *looks down and notices that she is still holding the mask. She studies it. And then, slowly, her mouth opens and a sound starts to emerge – something like a wail, something like the sound of an animal in distress. She begins to tremble, her body is taken over by a sweeping surge of emotion, something that has been restrained and repressed for many years.*

Slowly, with difficulty, she recovers. She comes to stand in the middle of the room, clutching the mask against her chest and staring ahead.

Blackout.

The End.

www.nickhernbooks.co.uk

facebook.com/nickhernbooks

twitter.com/nickhernbooks